MANAGING PROJECTS WELL

Managing Projects Well

Stephen A. Bender

OXFORD • AUCKLAND • BOSTON • JOHANNESBURG • MELBOURNE • NEW DELHI

Butterworth-Heinemann
Linacre House, Jordan Hill, Oxford OX2 8DP
225 Wildwood Avenue, Woburn, MA 01801–2041
A division of Reed Educational and Professional Publishing Ltd

℞ A member of the Reed Elsevier plc group

First published 1997
Reprinted 1999, 2000

British Library Cataloguing in Publication Data
A catalogue record for this book is available from the British Library

ISBN 0 7506 4631 4

Printed and bound in Great Britain

FOR EVERY TITLE THAT WE PUBLISH, BUTTERWORTH-HEINEMANN
WILL PAY FOR BTCV TO PLANT AND CARE FOR A TREE.

Preface

This intensive look at project management teaches people what they need to know to lead or be members of a project team. This highly unusual treatment discusses the real world of projects. Perhaps it should be subtitled 'what they don't teach you in most project management schools'. Because it deals with people, this is a relationship-based project management approach.

Most project management texts deal heavily in technical areas alone, leaving participants ill-prepared for the real project world; I know I was. I found my past project management training, although thorough and technical, to be only about 5% of what I needed to know. I have learned these lessons the hard way, and wish for others not to have to do the same. This book spends less time in traditional technical areas, with most time spent in the behavioural areas of project management and team participation.

My experience includes many years of project membership and management, and simultaneous projects, ranging from the small to the multi-million dollar size. After examining the vast array of project management books, this publisher has found my approach so unique and important that they asked me to author this book.

Recommended readers are people who will either lead projects, or be team members or their managers. It also includes secretarial or administrative personnel who often have to juggle many projects at one time. Detailed subjects include:

- what happens when your boss decides the project's schedule and budget and you have to work backwards to make things fit!
- how to communicate and present effectively within and beyond the team;
- how to cope when you do all the work, and have to manage multiple projects and non-project time besides;
- dealing effectively with stress;
- managing your time effectively and planning your day—without leaving your family behind;
- changing your unproductive habits—quickly;
- what to do when things go wrong, and planning for it, including late suppliers, unannounced vacations, people quitting or being pulled to another project, budget cuts and schedule accelerations; and

- organising people for success, including ideal methods for team member motivation. This includes the work effectiveness model.

Of course, traditional technical areas of project leadership are covered as well, including planning, organising, leading, and controlling a project. Even these technical elements are sculpted here for the real world of projects: project tasking and work breakdown structures, estimating, and scheduling using CPM, PERT and GANTT techniques. The book includes reporting on project status and organising for success.

I know you will benefit (the easy way) from reading about these techniques as much as I did from discovering them (the hard way). May you have a productive and enlightening journey.

Stephen A. Bender
Englewood, Colorado, USA

Contents

SECTION 4 What they don't teach you in project management school

Acknowledgements

It is important to me to acknowledge some of the many players who have made this work possible. I send my thanks to:

- my wife Charlene, whose guidance in my projects and intuition on relationship-based techniques was most helpful;
- my publisher, who had the wisdom to see this as a completely different approach and approached me to write it;
- my editor, Brendan Atkins, who enjoyed practising the techniques in this book during his tireless work;
- the people at Tele-Resources, Inc., whose combinations of hardware and software projects and 'nitty-gritty' detail taught me how to manage my time technically;
- many individuals at Key Banks, Inc., whose 'saturation bombing' of multiple projects forced me to develop special techniques to not only be effective yet to stay sane;
- General Electric Corporate Research and Development, whose strong interest in a 'people first' approach to project management launched this work in workshop format;
- my many consultancy and training customers around the world, who helped me tune my views to various industries and cultures.

And to you, the reader, who shares in this experience and puts these principles into practice.

For permission to use the swish technique, I thank Linda Sommer of the Eastern NLP Institute (c/o CommTech Group, 1251 Eagle Rd, New Hope, PA 18938). Thanks also to Dorset Press and Greenwood Press.

section

About projects and quality

1　A new view of concepts

As I mentioned in the Preface, I was woefully unprepared for the real world of projects. My formal training was excellent: it covered almost 5% of what I needed to know! In my 'trial by fire' I learned the other 95%—the hard way. It is this view that I share in this work.

The success of projects depends on many things:

- understanding what a project is and what it isn't;
- knowing clearly the shared vision and tasks for project managers, project leaders, team leaders, and project team members;
- knowing excellent project management techniques; but you must also know what constitutes an excellent product of the project;
- closing the gap between what you say and what you do. To 'walk the talk,' you must first get your own affairs in order by managing time and stress, and using planning models;
- working well with others: one-on-one, meetings, facilitation, motivating, problem solving, status reporting, handling criticism or conflict, and delegating;
- being flexible and creative, and
- getting the requirements right.

Finally, you need to have a model to deploy these principles progressively, rather than overdoing it and then quitting.

Well, this seems like quite a bit. In fact, item by item, each of the things discussed in this work are things that you already know something about. Hopefully (except for certain specialised techniques) you will not learn one new thing about projects that you do not already know in some other context. Our purpose is to organise what you already know and put it into a plan of action. This work is not simply a compendium of human resources training materials, it is that subset of knowledge and techniques specifically involved in projects. Once again, if I had this information organised for me on my initial journey, life would have been much simpler. Therefore, let us take a look at the main concepts.

WHAT IS A PROJECT, ANYWAY?

A project is an organised effort to a specific, typically one-time, goal. We will be looking at projects not only in business but also personally, including home life, raising a family—even self-improvement.

It is important to understand what a project is and what it is not.

There are many things that go on in a company, or even in a household, that one does not consider to be projects, for example:

- ongoing operational work, or day-to-day repetitive actions. The structure of the work is known, typically via a series of procedures. While the content may differ, the actions to carry out the content are the same, such as running routine errands, making a meal, or seeking family entertainment;
- customer service actions, once designed, are not projects so long as the work is routine; and
- manufacturing assembly line operations on the shop floor, where the work does not change, even though different cars, machines, or parts are produced.

A project, by contrast, has a specific beginning and an end. In many important ways, no two projects are the same:

- a project has a specific goal. Once the goal is achieved, the project is over;

- a project is finite—it has a specific time period and an end point;

- a project is usually fairly complex and has many details;

- projects are generally one homogeneous unit. Even though large projects often have many phases, components, or sub-components (sub-projects), they form one unit overall; and

- in contrast to repetitive, day-to-day ongoing operations, projects tend to be one of a kind and non-repetitive.

Illustrations of projects include:

- software development activities. While there may be a uniform development methodology, the work might not be repetitive or operational. This is because the nature of the product being developed is different each time. However, the mass reproduction of user manuals or packaging of products such as diskettes or compact disks are not considered to be projects;
- the development of a new or unique machine tool in a job shop operation. Each machine tool is different, and when it is done, it is done;
- the development of a painting by an artist. The development and painting is a project; the mass production of multiple lithographs of the painting is not;

- the design of procedures used in day-to-day customer service operations by bank tellers, help desk attendants or operators, but not the day-to-day operations themselves. While the tasks in the procedure are repetitive, the initial design of the methods is not;
- a research and development activity, even if it leads to an idea rather than a finished product. The nature of the research is different each time, and it results in a specific outcome;
- planning a family vacation to a new or unusual destination—it is neither routine nor repetitive;
- gaining and using a new skill, or completing on-the-job training;
- undertaking new personal growth and introspection with a specific improvement goal in mind; and
- undertaking a major home improvement activity.

A final example: a custom home builder undertakes a project each time they build a new home. Although they may have constructed many homes, each home and each set of circumstances is different.

Products and processes

As we can see from the comparisons, any time you construct a new type of 'product' you are running a project. For the purpose of understanding this, we need to define what is meant by 'product'.

A product is the output of a process. It is not necessarily physical, or even tangible. If a process is an activity, or work, or an action, then a product is the result of such an action. As such, a product can, of course, be a physical thing that is constructed (a home, a piece of software, a machine tool). Because it is the output of a process, a product can also be a customer service action, a meeting, or even a thought—anything that is the result of an activity.

What defines a project is not the product. It is, instead, the fact that the product is unique and non-repetitive.

Some time ago, the content of this book was conveyed in workshop form to a large scientific research and development organisation. One of the participants questioned whether or not their work was a project. 'After all', he said, 'we don't actually make anything'. What he meant was, his work and that of his team, after research, resulted in a single idea—an idea for the consumer product that could be built using the technology embodied in the research. This idea is actually a product, because it is the result of a process (thinking and research). The fact that it is not tangible does not matter. Because of the nature of the research, the work done and the resultant idea is unique, non-repetitive, has an end point, and is expressed as one homogeneous unit. Therefore it is a project.

Project cascading and size

Many times, the output of one project (the product) is the input to another (part of the other's process). For example:

- the research and development activity results in an idea, and this is one project;
- the idea is then used to build a prototype of a new customer product. This activity is a project also;
- the prototype is used to design the operations for the method of mass production on the manufacturing shop floor. The setup of the assembly line, for the first time, and the 'working out of any bugs' in the manufacturing operation, is also a project;
- the continued mass production of the customer product is not considered to be a project; and
- any subsequent quality assessment or focus group activity to validate that the product meets the needs of the market and customers is a project.

If projects are all different, how can it be possible to have any kind of a method to make their construction more efficient, effective, and of higher quality? Because although what 'goes through' a project activity is different, the techniques, activities and problems associated with vastly different projects can be very much the same. In the same way that a software development project can be governed by a phased methodology that remains the same, so too can projects be governed.

This 'same kind of things' approach applies not only to the technical aspects of project management, but also to the human side: staying 'sane', managing stress levels, managing your time, leading your people, and being a quality participant in the process as a team member.

Projects can be 'phased'; that is, broken down to a series of sequential steps. They can also have concurrent sub-elements or modules. These pieces can be very small projects in themselves. For example, many job-shop operations, such as software projects, require sequential developmental phases (requirements, design, construction, testing, and implementation). Also, many complex projects need to be broken down into smaller pieces just to make them manageable. The planning of an extensive family vacation might have concurrent pieces done by different family members: selecting the vacation spot, meeting the needs of all family members, planning travel arrangements, booking reservations, completing office work and cross training others for your absence, allocating savings to finance the trip and expenses during the trip, and so forth.

On the other hand, projects can be very large. For example, I met the person responsible for laying all of the fibre optic cable in the ground, in the whole world, for a long distance communications company. This person had hundreds

5

of project managers working for him. In a sense, his 'project' was to coordinate the projects managed by his team members.

Now that we have an idea of what constitutes a project, let's take a look at the players...

A DIFFERENT VIEW OF LEADERS, MANAGERS, AND EMPLOYEES

Many discussions on projects fail to take into account:

- the actual roles of the project manager;
- the difference between management and leadership;
- additional responsibilities of the project manager; and
- the significant role of the project team members.

The role of the project manager

The project manager, in traditional project management tutorials, is the one who plans, organises, and controls the project. Perhaps it should be stated that the project manager plans, organises, *leads* and controls a project. If assigned this role, you must accomplish your goals through the efforts of others.

The 'planning' piece occurs initially, before the project is actually underway by the team members, and may have to be repeated during the project, especially if there are changes along the way.

The 'organising' piece involves allocating equipment, resources, people, money, suppliers, and anything else that is necessary to run the project, based on the plan. This frequently involves coordination with others.

The 'control' piece essentially means the comparison of the plan with the actual progress, and making any necessary 'mid-course' corrections. This is an often overlooked area of most projects. In quality terms, the planning piece is 'prevention' based; that is, it guides the project in the proper direction, and prevents subsequent failures if properly done. The control piece is 'correction' based; that is, it identifies variations of the project with the plan, and re-plans based on actual circumstances. Technically, it is true that prevention is more powerful, and better than, correction, if a choice had to be made.

Yet in the real world, it is almost necessary to be better at project controls than project planning, if you were forced to make a choice. Seldom do projects go exactly as planned. The very fact that a project includes elements that have not been done before (by definition) means that there is a certain element of unpredictability, no matter what planning is done.

Many people erroneously plan projects in great detail, omitting contingencies, and then fail to control them. When they notice that the project has gone awry, they simply abandon the plan and 'shoot from the hip'. The result is an ad-hoc approach to project management with resultant cost overruns, missed dates, and poor quality projects.

While I cannot advocate lack of planning, a person who plans but does not control is in worse shape than a person who controls without planning. In the latter case, at least the project is continuously re-oriented to the real-world facts and events of the day. Obviously, both planning and control are necessary. It is hard to overemphasise the importance of adequate project controls because this is an extremely common failing in projects.

Think of it this way: it is important to be able to predict, or forecast, the weather (planning). We might not want to go for a day trip with the family if rain is forecast, although we would if it were sunny. However, if the weather forecast was fair, and we were at a ball game, we would probably cancel it if a heavy downpour ensued (control). It would not matter what was forecast: it is the reality that would affect our behaviour. In fact, the good project manager 'prepares for rain' even if the forecast is clear. In essence, the actual weather (rain or shine) is 100% accurate in the moment, while the forecast may be inaccurate. For a project, the reality that a certain task did not complete in time is a 100% certainty in the present, while the prediction that it would or would not complete in time is not 100%.

The issue at hand is usually the ego of the project manager, wishing through 'habituation' or 'cognitive dissidence' that the prediction would come true, even in the face of conflicting real outcomes. We are so blinded by past experience (habituation) or invested in our plan with 'tunnel vision'(cognitive dissidence) that we think controlling our projects is an admission of failure. It is not—it is an admission of wisdom!

This, then, is planning, organising, and controlling—the P-O-C of projects. This is the 5% of project knowledge and experience. At the beginning of this book, I suggested that there was another 95%. Part of this is:

- leading and motivating others; and
- doing actions through the work of others (delegating).

So, project management is planning, organising, leading, and controlling, all while properly motivating and delegating. These two new areas are the 'forgotten children' of many project managers. It is very odd that most treatments on project management describe the start-up (planning, organising) and corrections after completion of tasks (controlling), but not what happens during the execution of the project (running the project, or leading). How well this is done can make or break projects. And to try to do everything yourself can be most disappointing indeed.

Try to imagine a family in which a parent plans a vacation, organises all the details, and is there to control the finances after completion, and is not present during the vacation and does not actually go! This is absurd, yet is attempted with many projects in the office. Also, try to imagine the man who managed the fibre optic cable project mentioned above. How well would this have worked had he tried to do the entire job himself?

Many technicians in specialty fields are rewarded by their managers with project management positions. They are taught the P-O-C of project management, and then 'thrown to the wolves' to fend for themselves in such a position. Of course, they don't know how to do that. The natural result is this: they reward themselves by choosing all the great tasks for themselves. This gives them a feeling of accomplishment. Since it is easier to tell when you are done with a technical task then when you are done with a management initiative, there seems to be more 'completion'.

The fallacy with this thought is twofold. First, a detailed task might be taking time away from your project management responsibilities. Second, by taking the interesting tasks for yourself, you are 'robbing' others of the exciting work, decreasing their motivation, and possibly sending the signal that they are not trusted.

It is true that there are many kinds of projects: large ones for which the project management position is full-time, where a number of people are doing the detailed tasks, and smaller projects for which you are the only team member—both project manager and team member, 'doer' of all tasks. Even more, you might be managing several projects, either doing management tasks alone or managing/doing coupled with other projects and non-project activity.

One cannot cast a rule for delegation in stone. It is sometimes necessary for you, the project manager, to do certain tasks for which you are the only one having the expertise (especially in smaller projects where it is simply a necessity to do the detailed work too). The test is this (and this is the secret question you need to answer for yourself honestly, perhaps privately):

- Have I done all the planning, organising, leading/running, and controlling that really needs to be done, or am I skipping this work to do the task?
- Am I selecting the task only because I enjoy it, for my own ego, or to get a sense of completion? Or am I doing it because it is indeed an appropriate way to use my time?

You know the answers! Don't hesitate to ask yourself the questions!

The difference between management and leadership

Projects need to be managed, yet people need to be led. In other words, work needs to be managed, yet people never do. In accordance with modern quality principles clearly expressed by (for example) W. Edwards Deming and the Malcolm Baldrige National Quality Award, work needs to be planned, organised, and controlled, yet people should not. Many people confuse these two issues.

Therefore, the enlightened, empowered project manager is actually a project leader. Some companies for whom I have conducted workshops have asked for the course to be renamed 'Project Leadership' for that very reason. A leader empowers others and gets consensus, delegating the work and important pieces of the project management areas as well. This improves the sense of involvement, commitment, and esprit-de-corps of team members as well.

Leaders catalyse others into action and establish a clear vision for what is desired. They take the joke 'do what I say, not as I do' and turn it around into 'do what I do, not what I say'. They trust that you know how to do the work. They describe what to do, and leave the how up to you. They control the work, not the worker. This is truly a quality person.

To take the work personally, such as finding fault or laying blame, is part of a manager's flawed attempt to control how the work is done. It de-personalises the team member, the one doing the work. To look at work impersonally (not as my work or your work, but instead as the work) without blame, depersonalises the work and empowers the individual once again. This is the way that two friends on a team would look at the problem or issue or task, and work together to solve or resolve it—looking at the work, not the worker. Another way of putting it:

- personalising the work depersonalises the worker;
- depersonalising the work personalises the worker.

We want the last bullet, not the first! That is what a leader does.

In industry, the terms 'project manager', 'project leader', and 'team leader' all have slightly different meanings that vary from organisation to organisation. Often, 'project leader' emphasises the leadership aspect rather than management; it also sometimes depicts a role subordinate to the overall project manager on the same project for complex multi-tiered projects. The term 'team leader' often is used to refer to the leader of a sub-piece of a project. Since the leadership principles are the same, and the work description is the same, we shall use these terms interchangeably. This is even more appropriate given the premise that we propose project team members should try to walk in the shoes of the project manager. In a sense, the team leader is a project team member of an even bigger project and needs to walk in the shoes of the overall project manager.

Additional responsibilities of the project manager

As will be seen in subsequent detail, the project manager makes contributions by:

- communicating well with all team members, and members of functional management. In family and personal situations, this includes explaining the reasoning behind your actions, and seeking ownership, endorsement, and contribution of others;
- defining what is in the scope of the project and what is not (the project's boundaries);
- reporting on the intermediate and final project outcomes to supervising functional and executive management;
- scheduling the work, and helping team members to properly estimate the duration of the work tasks;
- avoiding at all costs instilling fear in the hearts of team members, which may cause them to be reluctant to report exceptions.

And by:

- being a good politician;
- being a great motivator; and
- being highly involved.

The significant role of the project team member

Perhaps over half of this book applies to project team members: those who may not lead or manage a project, yet have responsibilities for accomplishing the tasks.

One role, the obvious one, is to carry out the work in the assigned task—yet this is one of only six roles. In most projects, people assign only this first one and forget the other five that make the difference. Here are the roles:

- Do the detailed task
- Be a team player
- Report exceptions
- Estimate the work yourself
- Anticipate needs of other members
- Walk in the project manager's (and other team member's) shoes

1   Do the detailed task.
We won't say a lot about this first one because it is covered by so many excellent texts on project management. This is what everyone focuses on. Let's go to the forgotten areas.

2   Be a team player.
There are many groups, however few teams, in this world. Getting together a group of people and assigning them work as part of the same project hardly makes them a team—it makes them a group.

So what is a team?

Let's first describe what a group is. A group of people typically is a functional unit organised by decree to work together on tasks for a project (in this case). Most notably, groups get together to understand assignments, then go off individually to perform them. They usually minimise interactions except where absolutely necessary and work as 'islands' perhaps out of synchronisation with others. They are off in their world, solving problems and constructing solutions, without true awareness of the challenges or issues of others. This is the true nature, unfortunately, of most project 'teams' that are really 'groups'.

Groups do not function very well. There is no team synergy, nor is there awareness of the issues of others, nor is there the benefit of many getting together to solve problems. There is even the sense of one saying to another, 'Well, that's your problem'. For sure, resources can be improperly allocated, with late or missed deliverables happening to the complete surprise of others.

Teams, on the other hand (the way I like to define them) consider that one person's problem is everyone's problem. There is genuine interest in each member being intimately familiar with the problems, issues, and timetables of another in the team. Because of the considerable interest in working together, there is no such thing as a 'surprise' late deliverable, or one piece not fitting into another.

Teams are mandatory for the successful execution of projects.

3   Report exceptions.
A good team member (not a group member) understands deeply how important it is to report to other team members, and especially the project manager, upcoming troubles with his/her aspect of the project. This could include supplier difficulties, hardware problems, confusions, missing dates, going over budget, and the like.

This is easier than it sounds. A true team member understands the importance of this because they are members of a team, not a group. In addition, no project manager likes surprises—having lots of contingencies and hearing bad news is far superior to being surprised. So why is this so hard?

In a traditionally hierarchical organisation, where fear often predominates, it is common to worry about consequences of reporting delays or problems in projects. What if my boss thinks I am inadequate? Will I get fired? What does this say about my inability to estimate timetables, costs, or contingencies?

Since we are talking about leadership rather than management, a good leader invites both customers and employees to complain. They do this realising that their people know far more about how to get the work done than they do.

Therefore, you as a project team member must realise that, hard as it is, it is better for the project to admit a shortcoming than to hide it—after all, it is the work, not the worker, that is of concern.

Equally important, it is imperative that you, as the project leader, make it easy for your team members to report these exceptions without fear. Just put yourself in their shoes—how would you want to be treated?

4   Your own estimating.

As a team member, it is important to do your own estimating of the tasks, in terms of its length, cost, needed resources, equipment, suppliers, and so forth. You also need to know how to do this well; Section 4 gives you a new method for estimating. Your project manager can give you the tools and the encouragement you need—and not your estimate.

Why is this?

Consider this illustration: I know someone who, having left home as a teenager, decided she knew everything about how to live on her own. Armed with a part-time job, yet full-time school, full-time tuition, full-time car payment, full-time car insurance, full-time rent, full-time food bill, and again, part-time job, she tried to make it on her own. She had apparently read one of those signs that said: 'Teenagers! Leave home now while you still know everything' and thought it was serious! (Of course, the sign was written in jest. However, if you doubt that teenagers know everything, just ask them!)

After several months out on her own (with the last two weeks probably living on soup and ketchup sandwiches), she came back home and reported, 'Do you know how much a carton of milk costs?'.

That 'someone' was our daughter! Of course we knew, since we had made the same comment to her when she left the milk out of the refrigerator to spoil. She barely remembers that. Yet she realises now, given the experience of having to do that purchase on her own. To think of it, I had much the same experience in my younger days, and remember making almost the same comment to my parents. They reported to me that they had reminded me of milk costs and spoilage when I lived at home, yet I could not honestly remember that either!

Our daughter had left home, and come back wiser, amazed at 'how much we had learned' while she was gone! Of course, in reality she was more aware of what we always knew.

What was the difference?

Ownership!

What is the point?

When a person experiences an activity personally, they remember it and change their behaviour. When they don't experience it, their behaviour does not necessarily change. It is not necessarily the case that they don't believe you—it is somehow more personal when it is experienced.

This is why a poor estimate constructed by the person that must follow it is better than the great estimate formulated by their boss.

Why?

Because you, the team member forming the estimate, have ownership of the estimate if you made it. If it is wrong, you will take steps to correct it and learn from it. If it is right, and the project manager made it, then you are not necessarily motivated to work to that estimate or endorse it, or even correct it.

5   *Anticipate needs.*
This is a detailed way of being a team player. It is what you need to do. By constantly thinking of the needs of the other person (the other team members) you can anticipate the deliverables (inputs) they need that you provide as products (outputs). If your timing is delayed or if there are problems, you will be the first to notify that team member so you can work together. You can then solve problems as a team and perhaps get the project back on track.

As a team member, you must anticipate the needs of the project manager as well. If you were the project manager what would you require? With full knowledge of the multiple tasks of the project, and of what the project manager is trying to accomplish, you can anticipate the needs and requests of the project manager without even asking, furnishing reports, data, and information even before requested. This makes the project manager's job much easier.

6.   *Walk in the other's shoes.*
If 'anticipate needs' is the 'what' you need to do, then this is the 'how'. To properly do this, you need to understand what it is like to 'be in their skin' or 'walk in their shoes'. A special exercise for doing this is covered in Chapter 9.

The better you can imagine what it is like for the other person, be it a team member or project manager, the better you will be able to relate. By the way, this is an important skill for project managers to have as well!

Most communication problems result in one person forgetting what it is like for the other person. In fact, most quality problems with products, services, and projects originate from this forgetfulness.

SUMMARY OF TECHNICAL CONCEPTS

It is appropriate to describe in some depth, yet highlight, the technical aspects of project management—the 5%—that project management texts and schools would like you to believe is the 100% you need to know.

The technical skills outlined in Section 4 are indeed important. In fact, they are mandatory prerequisites to running a project well. It is simply a fact that these skills are necessary, but not nearly sufficient.

They include planning, organising, running and controlling a project.

Planning includes:

- techniques to select which project to do;
- methods to define what is in the project and what is not (scope);
- ways to break down the work into smaller chunks, called tasks. You may also need to identify the types of resources that are required, such as personnel;
- procedures to estimate the time needed for both the entire project and each individual task. These procedures must include estimates for resource consumption (personnel and money), both general and detailed;
- means to schedule the work so that tasks are started and ended by certain dates. An estimate is not a schedule. An estimate prescribes how long, and a schedule prescribes by when. One cannot divide estimates, in person-months, by the number of available people to get calendar due dates! Putting 10 people on the job to make a machine tool doesn't get the tool done in one-tenth of the time—it just creates 10 different machine tools!
- calculations of the cost and resource consumption based on the schedule, not on the estimates; and
- allocation of funding and resources based on this planning.

Note: even as a project manager, you have a person to whom you must report. Frequently, their ideas of project schedules and budgets do not agree with yours. Does that mean you abandon planning and go with their idea? No!

Planning involves going 'left to right' on the list of tasks: selecting, defining, breaking down work into tasks, estimating, scheduling, costing, and allocating resources. Your boss may prescribe the resource allocation, costing, and scheduling, setting up a 'right to left' task sequence! You must in fact deal with both directions, and both your ideas and those of your manager are reasonable.

For example, you may have calculated the most efficient and effective way to do a project. Your management, however, may have determined that 'time to market' and other necessary concerns have attached certain market benefit to the product. You have computed the project as taking 14 weeks with the stated resources. Yet, there is an industry trade show in 12 weeks, and the next show after that is a year away. The best product in the world won't sell if there are no buyers and no market. Both sides are right.

Unless you calculate when the project will be done using regular methods, you will be unable to determine which project paths to accelerate ('crash') in order to make the trade show. More costly? Sure! Cheaper than missing the market and having no sales? Of course! There is an optimum balance.

In the theoretical world of projects, you calculate schedules, resources, budgets, and tacitly get approval and proceed. In the real world of projects, your management dictates schedules and budgets and they are seldom what you calculate. You must be able to work well with both.

Organising includes allocating the people, suppliers, equipment, money, logistics, office space, and other details needed to 'turn the key' and start the project. This may entail considerable planning in itself. Where 'Planning' in the P-O-C model is the approach, then 'Organising' is the deployment. Good ideas (planning) plus good implementation (organisation) equals results. Both are needed.

As a quality examiner, I have seen examples of a great approach set in motion by a company, with no implementation and minimal deployment. If one area of a company only is following a great plan, then its effect on the overall company is minimal. This is like a project plan with no organising. A frequent example is strategic plans known only to executives but not to individual departments; they are therefore not followed.

I have also seen examples of a fully deployed bad idea. A bad technique that is replicated throughout a company multiplies its badness! Frequent examples include improperly tested quality improvement initiatives or flawed business process re-engineering, that 'throw the baby out with the bathwater'. Such forgetfulness of what made a company great has caused business failures in two-thirds of companies that have attempted it.

Running or leading a project includes the day-to-day! Management By Walking Around! Not being stuck in your office! Watching for the snakes and alligators! Always leaving a 'back door' open and not closing your options!

As a commercial pilot having flown for an air taxi operator, I have come to practise 'always leaving a back door open'. This means keeping all of your options, and asking a lot of 'what if' questions.

At the US Army's Air National Guard Military Base on the airport where I did most of my flying, I once saw a sign: 'It is better to be down here, wishing you were flying up there, than to be up there, wishing you were down here!'. Wanting to be on the ground, of course, might happen if you, the pilot, failed to do proper weather planning, or did not check the aircraft properly and it failed in flight!

Controlling a project includes those actions to insure that the plan and the actual correspond to one another.

A thorough look at the consequences of controlling, and not controlling, a project was discussed earlier (see 'A different view of leaders, managers, and employees').

Elements of project control include:

- periodic (perhaps weekly) status reports by team members to compare projected completions versus actual;
- 'Management by Walking Around' to insure that people are working well with the tasks they have been assigned;
- monitoring time schedules and financial expenditures, headcounts, contingencies, suppliers, and 'back door' options;
- insuring that the end customers, as well as functional and senior management as needed, are familiar with the progress of the project.

SUMMARY OF BEHAVIOURAL CONCEPTS

This is the other 95% of what runs a project: behavioural, communication, management, and leadership skills.

Most matters are non-technical. It is necessary of course to understand technologies of projects: scheduling, PERT, CPM, and so forth. These are necessary, yet not sufficient, skills.

The preface to this book outlined many of the real-world skills required. Special skills are needed when someone quits, or becomes unproductive, or when other departments are against you. Still others are needed when dealing with multiple, colliding projects, cross-purposes, unworkable schedules and budgets, and unanticipated emergencies.

To deal with these, you need to manage human behaviour—yours! Only then can you work with others. To keep your own house in order, you need to understand what messages you are sending and receiving. You need to manage your allocation of time and keep stress under control.

And above all, you need a mentality of dealing with the world when things 'go wrong'. This includes leaving the back door open, mentioned above.

Electronic project tools are a limited answer. Not only do they deal with the '5%' piece, they only do a portion of that because:

- many software project tool training manuals mention that expertise in how to manage projects is assumed as a prerequisite;
- project planning includes project selection procedures; identifying the large then small pieces of work; estimating the length of the pieces; scheduling and costing the work; and then seeking approval and funding. Tools cannot select the project. Nor can they identify the work pieces, big or small, or even estimate how long they take. They also cannot decide for you which people have what expertise, or how long they would take, or their availability. These tools will, however, quickly show you a possible schedule and costing based on entered figures much faster than you could do it with a calculator. Once again, however, you are on your own for project approval and funding;
- project organising is done solely by you, based on information in the plan;
- no computer program tells you how to lead or run the project; and
- software is a great tool for recalculating networks to enable you to control the project. However, what you do about the amended forecasts is up to you. The impact of the decisions you make can be projected and made more rapid with software; no software will make decisions for you.

Software tools can make possible the impossible: you would not be thorough enough with scheduling if the tasks had to be scheduled by hand. Further, you would not be tempted to control projects very well, knowing the best way is to recompute the network each week to compare actual versus estimated. The overwhelming task of trying to do this by hand would probably prevent you from analysing how projects are going.

As you can see, however, these tools accomplish a small part of what is needed. Perhaps they are 20% of the 5% piece.

It is much like someone declaring you to be a carpenter, able to build houses, flats, or apartments, just because they gave you a hammer. House building is far more than hunting around for nails to hit with your new hammer. It is also exceptionally difficult to press nails in with your thumb!

Behavioural elements therefore include:

- getting your own house in order. This includes how you plan your day, how you manage your time in new ways, handling change, handling stress, and insuring message sent equals message received;
- leading others and running a project. This includes how you work 'one-on-one' with others; how you work with groups; how you motivate others; how you write; and how you handle dissension;

- manifesting the principles of quality throughout the project; and
- getting the right requirements and using creative techniques during project development.

Indeed, these elements constitute the majority of this book.

2 Building the product right

This chapter gives a special orientation to product quality—a necessary part of all worthwhile projects.

WHY IS PRODUCT QUALITY IMPORTANT?

It doesn't make very much sense to use superior methods to run a project if what you produce in the project is of very poor quality. Good methods do not automatically assure good products. With the knowledge of this chapter in mind, you can be sure that your methods are also oriented to building superior products.

MAGIC AND MISERY IN PRODUCTS AND PROJECTS

Let's take a look at some products and services in a non-business context.

A 'magic' moment is one where your experience is so overwhelmingly positive, it 'takes your breath away'. Instead of just being pleased with the product or service, its behaviour or performance is so outstanding it is unexpected. You not only tell others about the quality of the product or service, you tend to brag or even boast about it to other people.

A 'misery' moment is quite the opposite. Your experience is very negative: the product breaks down, or you get poor customer service. Keep in mind that a person who is really upset due to poor product or service quality will tell a lot of people about it—perhaps more people than they would for a moment of magic. It has been said that a person having a misery moment might tell more than 20 people about it.

Let's look at an example of misery.

An associate of mine had a bad experience with the US Postal Service. She went to mail a letter on a Saturday, when the post office was open. It was a beautiful building, a wonderful, Gothic, architecturally significant place. When she walked in, all the customer service windows were open, yet there was nobody there! Finally, a woman, somewhat dishevelled, chewing gum, came out from behind a door, and said, screeching: 'Whatd'ya want?' (Translation: 'What do you want?')

13 Institute a vigorous program of education and retraining to keep up with changes in materials, methods, product design, and machinery. ('Retraining' principle)

14 Clearly define top management's permanent commitment to quality and productivity and its obligation to implement all of these principles. ('Leadership' principle)

In projects, this means that a continual focus on the vision or mission of the project will prevent you from being 'scattered'. There is no limit to how good a job you can do. The quality will improve if you trust your people to do a good job without constantly peering over the shoulders; arrange proper training; and avoid having other groups check their work. People will be proud of their work and, because fear is absent, won't hesitate to tell you when something is going wrong.

Most notably, you as a project manager need to plan, organise and control projects, yet never need to plan, organise, and control people. The work needs to be planned, organised and controlled, but not people. They need to be led, championed, encouraged, and shown the direction.

Many people think that quality costs something. Quality saves money. For this reason we will now look at the cost of quality in projects and clear up confusion about definitions.

IS QUALITY REALLY FREE?

Much has been said—in the newspapers, radio, TV, conversations, everywhere—about the need for a reduction in waste and rework, and improvement in productivity and quality. Global competition makes this more than a 'nice thing to have': it has become essential for our very survival. Many organisations, business and government, have started using quality tools, building teams, and looking for quality improvement opportunities. And yet the most significant opportunities for improvement lie in two frequently untouched areas: the *analysis of the flow*, or process, of one's work today, and a concept called the *Cost of Quality*. It is the latter concept that we will deal with now.

The term *Cost of Quality* implies that producing quality products costs money. Does quality cost money? Yes! Does that mean the book entitled *Quality is Free* is a misnomer? No! Does quality save money? Yes! How can both of these things be true together? The answer to this question, if thoroughly understood, will solve for you perhaps the biggest misunderstandings about quality of our time.

I like to start with some definitions, since we can't get very far if we don't know what we are talking about! Quality has many definitions, ranging from beauty in an artistic sense, to quality of life, quality of products and services, improved productivity, and reduced waste and rework (the need to do the job over again). For this discussion, let us concentrate on just two: quality of design, and quality of conformance.

- Quality of design is the quantity of features and functionality present with a given product or service.
- Quality of conformance is the degree to which the product or service meets internal requirements and is fit for use by the customer (customer satisfaction).

Definitions of Quality

Quality of Design

- adds cost
- creative

Quality of Conformance

- requirements met
- fit for use
- saves money

Quality of design (sometimes called the quality of scope or function) reflects the number of features in a product or service that make it appealing and attractive to the customer. Some engineering disciplines use the same term to reflect how defect-prone the work is; however, that is not our meaning here. Clearly, it takes more time, work, and money to produce a product or service that offers more 'things' in it. Hence, this is the form of quality that costs money.

Whether it is the lawn mower that is self-propelled, a car with all the bells and whistles, or customer service with many features, a higher quality of design involves more cost. Do not ignore, however, the fact that you may have more people spending more money on these products, increasing profits beyond the increased costs. A highly satisfied customer base therefore can make the extra costs worthwhile.

Quality of conformance, on the other hand, is the extent to which we build those appealing and attractive products free of defects, and do it right the first time. The cost of rework (doing it right the second or third time) and associated testing is not a cost your customer is willing to pay you for. It almost always takes more time and effort to do something wrong, to discover it is wrong, and to fix it, than to do it right the first time. With respect to defects and failures: if you don't put 'em in, you don't have to get 'em out! You don't have to pay to make them, find them, or fix them. Therefore, this form of quality saves money.

Quality of conformance is the extent to which producers of products and services meet internal specifications and requirements (the internal view). It is also the extent to which customers are satisfied with those products and find them fit for use (the external view). The Maytag repairman commercial (who is always out of work) and the reliable car that never breaks down are examples. Notice that the reliability and extent to which things work properly (we call this being defect-free) does not depend upon the amount of 'bells and whistles', features, or functionality. It is a curious fact that, nowadays, people are willing to spend more money for a product that does fewer things and won't quit! This is true even though it costs us less to develop and build!

The definitions above are the background for our dilemma. Quality of design costs money, while quality of conformance saves money. When one person says quality saves, and another says it costs, both sides are right. Which kind of quality do you do? One? The other? Both? Consider this: if you build in quality of conformance, the money you save by doing it right the first time can be used to fund additional quality of design. For the same cost, therefore, you can build a more defect-free product that also has more features and appeals to the customer (and is more durable)! You can now manufacture a car that doesn't break down, and that has more options, for the same money. You can also offer more reliable customer service that doesn't go wrong, coupled with added services, for the same money.

Some people say that quality of design is the creative side of quality, and quality of conformance (standards, procedures, quality control, quality assurance) the more boring side. This is patently false. There is nothing boring about investigating causes of failure and creatively improving processes to eliminate them. Besides, if you invest no intentional time in quality of conformance, you will wind up spending all your time there! Time used to correct needless failures will steal time away from your creative quality of design time. So if you want to have more time for high quality designs and attributes of customer service, pay some attention to the needless waste and rework. You can use the time you save in building the reliable lawn mower to design a special grass catcher.

In the global marketplace, it is often said that North America has a high level of quality of design, and somewhat lower quality of conformance. This includes cars with electric antennas and electric windows that often break. (I am reminded of a woman who drove into the dealership in the pouring rain, with the driver's side window stuck in the down position. Her silk outfit did not fare too well in a water wash!) In other parts of the world, some countries have a lower quality of design, but a higher quality of conformance. Guess who's winning in the global market? Those with quality of conformance! Although not asked for very often, it is this form of quality that is actually a prerequisite to quality of design. People don't ask for it because they expect it. When a product breaks down, they feel betrayed.

Remember Maslow's hierarchy of needs? This has food, water, and shelter on the bottom as basic needs, and self-actualisation near the top. If you don't have food, you spend little time contemplating your navel. Quality of conformance (defects—food, water, shelter) and quality of design (features—self-actualisation) are related in a similar way. If you have defects in products and workmanship, it really doesn't matter very much what extra features you have.

Let's concentrate now on quality of conformance, since that is the under-used prerequisite. In times of corporate downsizing, where we have to do more with less, this is the kind of quality we need the most. It has been estimated that at least 20–30% of the Gross Domestic Product is spent on waste and rework (non-productive activities). Perhaps 7% of the GDP is waste attributable to failing software products alone! To track this, we begin by understanding it, in much the same way as a hunter needs to understand a wild animal in order to track it (where it goes, how it eats).

Here is a diagram of a *workflow model* to help with this understanding:

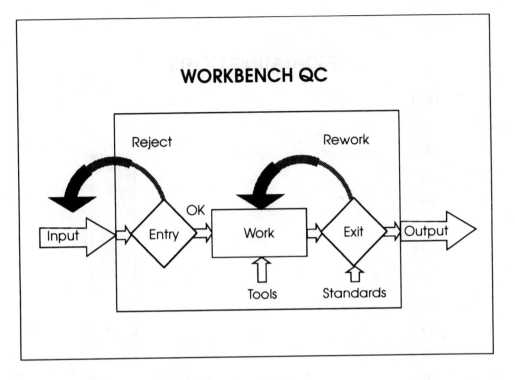

This quality model, called a workbench, shows us a way of categorising the work we do. Products and services coming in from a supplier are on the left; we do work using those products to create new or upgraded products, which pass to our customers, on the right. Incoming defective work should be returned (after all, the supplier is best at fixing those defects). We do the work, and then check the work. If our own testing of our work reveals defects, then products need to be reworked. Finally, only when our products are free from errors, do we pass them on to the customer (or the next workstation, hence the term, *internal customer.*)

If defects are passed from one person's 'workstation' or workbench to another, they are said to 'leak'. This principle is called defect leakage, and is expensive, since others are inconvenienced by delays and rework until input products are corrected. This has a cascading effect. Small errors early in a design, development, manufacturing or service flow process can lead to huge costs of correction later on. For example, in the following chart notice how inexpensive it is to correct an error during the requirements step. Correcting that same defect during implementation is much more expensive.

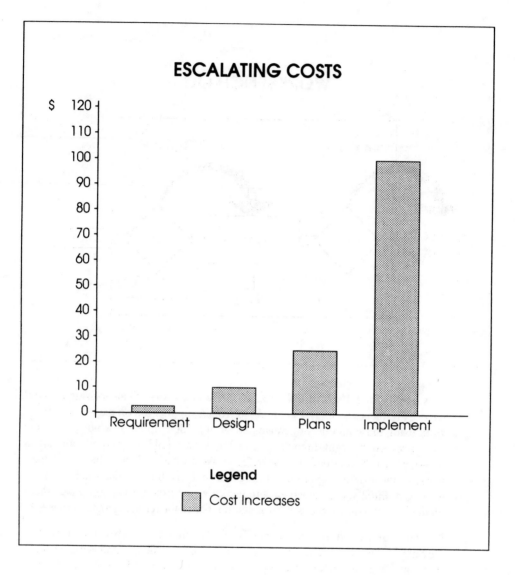

Can you imagine if we tolerated even a small percentage of defects in workmanship in the following areas? Here's what would happen if we were 99.9% defect free:

Acceptable quality level 99.9%

- **18 aeroplanes crash daily**

- **17,660 mail mix-ups hourly**

- **3,700 bad drugs dispensed daily**

- **10 dropped babies daily**

- **$24.8 million mischarged hourly in banks**

- **500 bad surgeries weekly**

This brings us to our major focus: the cost of quality. Let's start with a diagram, showing the old way of doing business on the left and the new way (with greater savings) on the right:

Example of Cost of Quality

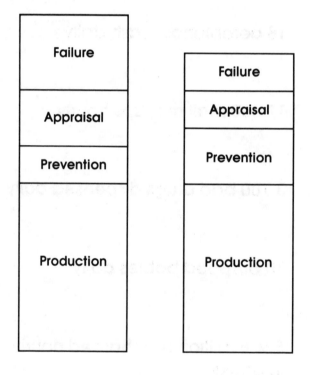

Failure is reduced when prevention is increased

This model shows, on the bottom of each side, the true cost of production. This is the cost of building the product or service, if we were to do it right the first time with no errors. (This is what our customers are paying us for.) It turns out that 'productivity' is the bottom half only; all other costs are 'unproductive' or wasteful.

The top of each side of the model is the cost of quality. Yes, even with quality of conformance, quality costs money. By changing the way in which our quality activities are divided, however, there can be a net saving (right side) compared to the old way of doing business (left side). Therefore there can be a 'return on investment' greater than the investment itself.

The cost of quality part of the diagram is divided into three parts: cost of prevention, cost of appraisal, and cost of failure.

The *cost of prevention* is any quality activity designed to help you do the job right the first time. It generally helps the next project, not the current one. It includes many activities often called 'overhead'. These activities are for the development of standards and procedures, measurement systems, and training programs; the cost of a Quality Assurance group; and process improvement methods and team meetings related to work improvements.

The *cost of appraisal* is quality control, or 'testing'. It is any activity designed to appraise, test, or check if the product you produce is defective. In manufacturing, this might be a mock-up or trial, or individual bench testing of component parts during or after assembly. In service, this might be a 'dry run' or pilot program of a new service offering. In software, this includes reviews, walk-throughs, inspections, and computer testing of programs. The cost of appraisal is incurred during the current project or production effort rather than the next one. If the cost of prevention is the cost of doing it right the first time, then this is the cost of doing it right the second time. If there were no defects, then there would be no need for this testing; however, if defects are likely, it is better to find them through testing (internal failure) than deliver broken products or services to the customer (external failure).

The *cost of failure* is the worst and generally the biggest. I call it doing it right at no time. To get to this stage, the cost of prevention must be inadequate to prevent the error, and the cost of appraisal insufficient to catch it. This is external failure. Unlike prevention, which is invested before a project starts, and appraisal, invested during the operation, failure occurs after the product is finished, usually at the most embarrassing time—such as when your customer is trying to use your product or service. Examples include rework during development, financial asset losses, lost time, inconvenience, bad press, loss of good will and loss of face, loss of market share, backlog and lost opportunity costs (because we are too busy fixing old problems to take new work in), the Hubbell telescope, the Chicago Flood, and most man-made catastrophes that hit the newspapers and embarrass companies, and on, and on.

Any activity that lowers the height of the upper boxes (cost of quality) on the diagram is quality of conformance and is called *quality improvement*. Anything that reduces the height of the lower boxes (production), making production faster and cheaper at the same defect rate, is called *process improvement*. Finally, anything that improves the quality of design (features and functionality) of the products or service is called *product improvement*. Clearly, our discussion on the cost of quality is about quality improvement.

Increased testing (appraisal) greatly reduces failure. However (and this is poorly understood), increasing prevention drastically reduces the need for both appraisal and failure. If you look at the right side of the diagram, you will notice that the sum of the reduction in cost of appraisal and failure is greater than the cost of increased prevention, resulting in an overall saving. In other words, this is where we need to put our quality dollars: quality improvement—defect prevention.

Strictly speaking, quality is not free, not even for quality of conformance. All three cost of quality components are unproductive costs. By changing the investment we make in each component, however, we can reduce them so that what we are doing is best for the customer. This is why the right kind of quality is free by comparison: prevention types of quality cost 'negative dollars' compared to the cost of failure.

When we get sick, that is failure. Having a doctor cure us so we don't get worse is appraisal. Engaging in a wellness and fitness program so we don't get sick in the first place is best, and is prevention. As a culture, do we focus more on appraisal and failure? Where should we spend our health care dollars?

When criminals steal, injure, and kill, that is failure. When they are caught and incarcerated, that is appraisal. Proper day care, family values, and programs that reduce the tendency for one to turn to crime are prevention-based. Are we spending our quality dollars wisely?

Societies accidentally reward citizens for failure without meaning to:

- When the plant employee fixes a major failure, she/he is a hero. What about the employee who develops a product that doesn't even fail in the first place? Are they rewarded more (as one would hope), or less?
- Do we call prevention programs 'overhead', simply because they appear to delay projects although greatly accelerating future ones?
- Are slogans like 'ours is not to reason why' helpful attitudes? Prevention-based work says 'Ours is to reason why' and that 'Monday morning quarterbacking' (ie having hindsight) is good. Here are some further good quality slogans: 'A stitch in time saves nine' and 'Penny wise, pound foolish'.
- Do beepers sometimes allow us to respond to a failure instead of addressing the problem? If we took those beepers away, and failures went unresolved,

would we tend to eliminate the root cause of failure instead? Or do beepers help us to make failure acceptable, keep it efficient, and hide its true colours and costs? Are beepers costs of failure?

- Many customer service departments find and fix problems. If there were no problems, would there be any customer service departments of that type? Are those customer service departments costs of failure?

- Are you asked to pay for a maintenance contract, which therefore rewards the manufacturer for failure?

Simple idea? A revolution in thought is required of most people. Perhaps half of your day is spent in cost of quality, with much of it failure. We often maintain massive infrastructures, meetings, and help-desks to make failure acceptable. Should we instead correct or eliminate these failures through prevention?

Look at the workbench again: activities in the WORK box, and their improvement, are prevention; those in the EXIT box are appraisal and quality control, and any defects passed through both boxes to the customer are failure. You can mentally examine your work and see the types of quality activities you do every day.

Here's an exercise for you that will work wonders. For the next month, during the drive home, take a daily mental inventory of how you spend your day. Is it production? Is it cost of quality, and of what type: prevention, appraisal, or failure? How much of your day is spent in each category? Be sure to be honest with yourself in labelling, as this aids in recognition. There is no censure: your work doing 'cost of failure' may be valuable at the moment but it is not a productive activity. You want to reduce the quantity of time you spend on unproductive activities, which will come by recognising where you spend your time.

By looking at how and where we spend our time and dollars, and even our quality dollars, we can cut unproductive time, waste, and rework. As a result, we can meet the challenge of global competitiveness head-on. By looking at the work, its progression through the workbench, and the cost of quality, we can make a major individual improvement in quality wherever we are. Whether or not our organisation has embarked on a quality journey, we can do this action personally—with personal benefits and pride of workmanship as the natural outcome as well.

HOW HAVE WE FORGOTTEN THESE LESSONS?

We have sometimes not remembered *what drives what in projects*.

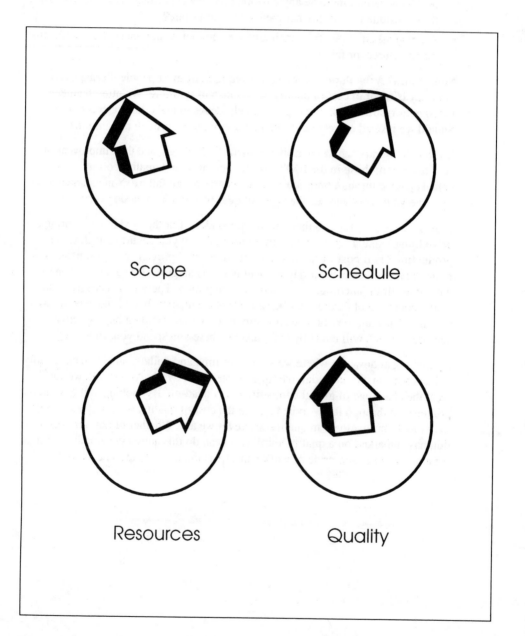

Scope

Schedule

Resources

Quality

This diagram shows the balance between scope, schedule, resources, and project quality.

Projects start out with a certain quantity of work assignment, or scope. The schedule and resources (budget, headcount, supplies, etc.) are often then set, and quality is often determined at a certain level. These four variables are interdependent. When one changes, the others change to compensate.

All goes well until something changes, usually scope. Does scope go down? Almost never! The scope of a project frequently increases. (By the way, this usually happens, not because the scope actually grows but because closer examination allows us to see its true size.) Typically, the schedule or resources don't change (but may be decreased). The result, because of these interdependent variables, is that the quality level is decreased.

The discussion we had in our introduction to quality and in the cost of quality clearly shows that enormous effort, time and money will be spent to correct quality problems not detected early on. In other words, the project will not finish within the assigned schedule and budget anyway. In fact, it will need to be enlarged far more than it would otherwise. It is better to consciously increase the schedule or resources, or both, to compensate for increasing scope, than pretend to leave them fixed because the schedule and budget would actually increase far less.

Since this is so obvious, why do intelligent men and women permit this illogical situation to happen?

The problem is that the schedule and resources are far better defined, unfortunately, than scope or quality. What gets defined gets done, measured and controlled.

If you were to march into your manager's office, delivering a project at the start of May, rather than the end of March when it was due, do you suppose the manager would be able to tell that it was overdue?

Of course! We don't get to say, 'Oh, I thought you were using the Aztec calendar'! We all know what a date is.

How about if you went over budget? Would the accounting department know that this had happened?

Of course! We don't get to say, 'Oh, I thought you were counting in foreign currency'!

Yet if we change the quality level, this is often harder to detect until later—and at the most embarrassing time—when the customer is trying to use our product. Until now, everyone defined quality differently. It was difficult to control because we did not know exactly what it meant. Our explanation above defines it quite specifically. By holding to that definition, the quality dial can be held firm if scope changes.

There is another very important dynamic that often causes poor quality: schedule and budget pressures.

Most accounting measurement systems measure apparent financial numbers rather than true cost or 'activity based' numbers. As a result, these flawed systems do 'project accounting' by 'costing' projects on resources utilised and time. Unfortunately, this happens *within* the boundaries of the project time frame.

It is possible, even tempting, to pass defective products on to the next phase or into production, simulating completion on or ahead of schedule or budget. In the short run, using project measures alone, this appears to save time and money.

The shortcut that saves a month can cost your company a year. Yet this added year is 'off the clock' and is not measured, too often, because the project accounting has ended. If we actually measured departmental activity, or cost, this would never happen. Also, if we 'charged back' to the project the higher costs of repair or maintenance due to sloppy workmanship, the true costs would be higher. I encourage each of you to use accounting systems that do not reward failure.

One other point: prevention-based activities (those that insure quality in projects) typically help the next project, not the present one. This is because the process improvements we design are often too late for the current projects, yet are valuable for the future. Shortcuts that appear to reduce schedule and resources seem to happen in the present, however. Traditional project financial accounting methods measure the present, not the future; no matter how much the future is corrupted, it will not be detected.

Consider the following multi-project diagram showing a sequence of four projects, each with a certain amount of good and bad quality in them. I will call these 'average' quality:

XXXXXXXXXX XXXXXXXXXX XXXXXXXXXX XXXXXXXXXX

Now, let's extend the length of the first project with an added prevention-based quality process, labelled QQQQQ. This process will shorten the length of future projects by an XXXX amount of time because future failure will be reduced.

Old: XXXXXXXXXX XXXXXXXXXX XXXXXXXXXX XXXXXXXXXX

New: XXXXXXXXXXQQQQQ XXXXX XXXXX XXXXX

Notice that the overall time for completing all four projects is less in the high quality (new) example than the average quality example (old). Quality saves time and money.

Notice, however, that any project accounting measure of time for the first project would seem to show that it takes longer and costs more money. This can lead you to avoid the quality process, which would have saved your company money in the long run.

Sometimes the 'long run' is not that long of a run!

Consider what happens if you plan a trip in your car or taxi, and you don't know where you are going. You can just start driving, use the wrong route, go back, and get there many hours late, because you 'saved time' not checking the map. Or, you can spend a few minutes planning the trip, and get there on time. The principle is exactly the same.

What would happen to our family vacation under the same conditions? You could arrive at your destination, with no plans of what to do when you got there. This is certainly spontaneous, and there is indeed a place for that. However, what would happen if you got to the ocean, and had packed no bathing suit? What if you took no money, and needed to stay at a hotel? What if you went to an amusement or theme park, only to discover it was closed on the day you planned to go? Planning does not mean rigidity, it means options—always leaving a 'back door open'.

To get through our project in a quality way, it will be necessary to make sure we are a model of performance for others.

2 Getting your own house in order

This section handles the primary prerequisite for being a good project manager, or even a good team member: how to manage yourself, 'getting your own house in order'. This is a large section because success begins and ends with you.

There are many familiar idioms that you may have heard related to this idea. They include 'You can't get another's house in order until you get your own house in order' or even 'People in glass houses shouldn't throw stones'. The latter means, of course, that you are not in a position to critique (or lead) anyone else until your own performance is a model for them to follow. The joke 'Do as I say, not as I do' just does not cut it in business or even in families.

Young children learn at an early age to quickly disregard anything that their parents say, and react and respond only to feelings and behaviours. In a sense, adults are much the same way. We can pretend that this does not make a difference, yet when we tune into our responses, we find that we model the behaviour of others as our first preference. In other words, we are more 'sophisticated' about it than children; that is, we 'lie' about its impact on us!

Haven't you ever heard someone telling you 'the right things' and something seems not quite right, or doesn't quite fit? Perhaps we are listening to a person saying out of integrity what they are supposed to say when they do not believe it themselves. What we hear is very logical, and yet in some cases we 'sense' a mismatch between beliefs and behaviours. With some of us, it can actually lead to a strong feeling of being sick to our stomach!

If you look at those people who have been most influential, perhaps those that are mentors, we find that it is the manager or project manager that shows by example rather than words that is most powerful.

As a result, this section focuses on a range of techniques used by successful people who are worthy of such mentoring. They are the very techniques I used during a period of multiple, large, parallel projects. Whether you lead projects or simply need to 'stay sane' while delivering project tasks as a team member, these techniques are for you.

Parents, and even children, can learn a lot from applying the techniques of managing time and stress, and even the general planning model described below.

The key areas are:

- Managing time, a new way
- General planning
- Dealing with change
- Your real self
- Handling stress

Let's look at them one by one.

3 Managing time, a new way

Much has been written on time management in the literature; our treatment here is intended to describe only those aspects relevant to projects. In addition, we want to forego the traditional methods that would have you turn into an 'efficiency expert' or 'automaton', and perhaps forget your family or other things really important to you in the process.

Stephen Covey, in many of his books, workshops, and speeches, makes a very useful point about the old and the new methods of managing your time. Although the principles I mention have been derived independently of his work, many have great similarity to his discussions. I encourage you to refer to his works as powerful supplementary reading in this area.

The most important thing to realise is that life is far more than sorting tasks out at work. The excellent business organiser, who cannot leave the office at the office, bringing work home with him or her, and has no family life because they are 'workaholic'—in what way are they excellent? Or, if you 'master' projects only to fail to achieve your important personal goals—how does this make you masterful? Would people really respect and appreciate you under such circumstances?

The well-balanced professional seems well balanced to others, and is easier to talk to, easier to negotiate with, and is more successful with suppliers, customers, and team members alike. Team members who have this balance are also much more of a pleasure to do business with. And, as a parent, because you are happy, your family is happy and goal-centred. Even children who practise some of these principles have an easier time in life and are more harmonious with the family.

Covey considers that the most modern, or fourth generation, time management approach is the one placing relationships and roles first, and understanding the balance between 'urgent' and 'important'. To use his words, 'the main thing is to keep the main thing, the main thing'. One of his books even says it in the title: *First Things First*.

The previous generation of time management, the third generation, was efficient and effective indeed, and not necessarily relationship-based. It embraced daily planners, logs, organising, and studies. Indeed, these are important and will also be summarised here. The fourth generation takes a close look at urgency compared to importance, which is especially crucial for success.

URGENCY AND IMPORTANCE

An urgent thing is time-sensitive. There can be many urgencies in projects, and many things that go wrong if their time-sensitive nature is ignored. Indeed, if my memory serves, the project manager of that very large fibre optic cable project had one critical path that would cost $US25 million for every *second* it was late! I think you would call that urgent!

Just because something is urgent, it is not automatically the most important thing in your life. Getting your time sheet in on time may be urgent, but not as important as getting the requirements right in the project.

Let's look at the notion of importance. Something that is important is a major segment of your personal or professional life; this is something that is part of your personal 'mission'. (Of course, if you don't have a sense of purpose, vision, or mission in your life, you may not be clear on what is important!) What is important can often be lost in the 'clutter' of life, including business life.

It may be important to handle this 'clutter' urgently and get it out of the way, and yet it is more important to devote the largest segment of time to those things that really matter: building an excellent customer product, furthering your professional goals, being a model for your family, and the like. It may be urgent to see that your family gets to school on time or meets an appointment, however it is important to have good family time, to teach good values, to keep members from addictive substances, and to instil in them a sense of purpose, for example.

So in summary, urgent things are time-sensitive, and yet may not be important. Usually, it is a good idea to do urgent things early, or at least timely, and to spend a minority of your time on them. Important things make a major difference in your life, whether or not they are urgent. You may not always do important things first or very early, and yet the majority of your time should be spent on these activities. The following statements are about 80% right, even if too simplistic:

- Urgent: do now (or timely), spend least time
- Important: do later (not too late), spend most time

Quite clearly, there are four combinations of these variables: things that are only urgent or important, things that are both, and things that are neither.

In life, most people respond automatically to urgent things. If they are also important—great! right things are being done. A job interview for a pre-planned career change is such an example. The career change is important, because it is part of your master plan to 'do what you love', and, as part of that plan, it is urgent that you are on time for a related job interview. However, we also respond just as quickly to those urgent things that are not centrally important to our personal mission, even though the world likes to label them as important: filling out our time sheet, paying bills on time, and the like.

Unfortunately, people do not automatically respond to important things, especially when they are not urgent. An example is the nagging sense that we want to advance our career and become a project manager in addition to being a team member, and have too much to do to pursue it. What about knowing that we want to spend more time with our family, but allowing these urgent project concerns to make us work late so that we just can't seem to do it? Same thing!

Worse, we sometimes spend great amounts of time in areas that are neither! The non-urgent, unimportant 'tasks' might be gossip, burning up many hours at the television (often called 'couch potato' time), or just being immobilised.

Therefore, we don't usually have trouble paying attention to things that are both urgent and important. If our lives are well balanced, we don't usually hang out in the 'couch potato' zone either.

If we don't watch out, though, we will do the urgent, unimportant tasks first (that's OK) and place the majority of our time in those areas (that's not OK)! Non-urgent but very important life activities may also not be tended to. It is my belief that having life driving you (urgent) instead of you driving your life (important) over long periods gives a sense of frustration that leads you to increase the 'couch potato' (unimportant, non-urgent) time as an exasperated result.

If we look at the quality principles in Chapter 2, we can see an important parallel between prevention and failure (on the one hand) and importance and urgency (on the other).

Many things that are urgent (and unimportant) are examples of the world driving us. The *world* is demanding that we do a certain thing, by a certain time. Bad things will happen unless we take timely action. Being continuously late for our job will get us fired. Not showing up for a doctor's appointment for a serious illness may lead to health complications. Maybe we won't be paid unless we turn in our time sheet by a certain time. Our children will be badly disappointed if we don't get them to the game or the play on time, especially if they are part of the team or cast!

In a sense, we are *reacting* to the world by responding to the urgent. This is the same way we react to failure by taking urgent, emergency measures. It is often critical that we do this, yet we are reacting to the world, or reacting to failure.

Many things that are important (and non-urgent) are examples of us driving the world. To do this, we must plan, we must choose. No one is standing around making us do it—it is up to us. We are *proactive* to the situation. In quality terms, it is prevention based; it prevents errors and problems later on. It is, of course, much easier for most of us to be reactive than proactive, especially in our cultures. We don't have as many (if any) outside influences, reminders, or 'pressures' to carry out our deep, internal mission-based desires. If we count on the world driving us, our important areas will be left sadly behind.

In Chapter 2, it was suggested that prevention negates failure, and it applies to the next time you do the work task. So it is with important things. In fact, I would like to suggest, or postulate, a theory: perhaps most urgency (the urgent and unimportant) is a result of failure! Look at it closely. With proper planning, would the urgent have been urgent? Perhaps not! And most people would prefer not to run their lives by having the world run them with urgent tasks, day after day, taking most of their lives this way. That is, if they could only stop themselves! So here is a possible motivation. Instead of just trying to 'work harder' at balancing the ratio of urgent to important, why not realise this: when you focus on what is really important, not only are you shifting your focus, you are also decreasing the number of urgent things pushed in your face!

The talented project manager or team member responds in a timely way to the urgent, and spends most of his or her time on important project (and life) goals to reduce urgency. This minimises the surprises. The principle of 'leaving a back door' is a prevention-based, important task. In that case, even the emergency can be taken in stride.

The Royal Dutch Shell Oil company is an outstanding example of placing the important before the urgent in terms of time invested. As an excellent example of scenario thinking, they postulated different market situations well in advance of their occurrence. What would happen if prices went way up? What if they bottomed out? What if there was an oil shortage? Suppose there was an overabundance? By planning what they would do in each of these situations, without knowing exactly which one would occur, they were ready. During the sudden shortage of the 1970s, they were ready with their pre-planned scenario far more quickly than others—and became one of the largest oil companies as a result of that success.

In the context of project planning, then, it is important (not urgent) to have a plan, and not be 'married' to it. Have a plan of action, and also have multiple outcome scenarios or 'what ifs', to respond rapidly to dynamic situations. No one will drive you to this thinking, or make you do it, because it is important and non-urgent. As a result, however, you will have a rapid response to what would have been an emergency or urgent situation, turning the urgent into the routine.

STRENGTHS, AND AREAS FOR IMPROVEMENT

To put these principles into action, we must pay attention also to project management-based techniques of traditional time management, with a new twist: making it relationship based. This is first the relationship with yourself, and then others. Doing this well is important, and not urgent. Therefore, we focus on it! By understanding what you do well, and what are areas for improvement, you will be more effective at work and at home.

Look at this list of 'self statements' which may be very true of you (a strength) or perhaps you wish they were more true of you (an area for improvement). I like to call these 'areas for improvement' because it is more positive than 'needs' or 'weaknesses'. Indeed, these items are not reasons to feel bad; they are simply objective observations for your own self-improvement. So, be objective! (Or, have a friend score this for you if that is less biased.) This list is compiled from a variety of sources, including my own experiences. It is not necessarily *the* list, nor is it intended to be complete or comprehensive; it shows directions and tendencies only.

Please look at these statements, and think about them, and their truth for you, without writing or recording anything. Is it true of you, a strength? Could you use major improvement in that area? Do you perhaps fall somewhere in between?

1 I recognise that proper handling of my time, in a relationships-based way, is a valuable possession.

2 I live in the present as much as possible.

3 I know that relationships and roles are primary and that traditional 'efficiency'-based time management techniques are secondary.

4 I have a strong sense of purpose in my life, with values, vision, and a personal mission statement.

5 I accept responsibility for my own life, free of blame of others; I am not a victim.

6 I am proactive rather than reactive in my life.

7 I make things happen, not just watch them happen or not know what's happening.

8 I am in touch with my most important wants, needs and desires.

9 I change myself rather than expect to change the world or things outside my control.

10 I translate my wants, needs, and mission into well-defined goals and objectives, have a plan to carry them out, and really take action on that plan.

11 I make a non-obsessive 'to-do' list weekly that is based on relationships and roles and that supports my mission, of which I am the driver. Daily alterations are minor compared to the weekly plan.

12 I have a list of those things that I might get to, which does not clutter those things that are important or that I must get to.

13 I clearly distinguish between things that are urgent and those that are important, with most time spent on important things.

14 I notice if, and why, I am doing excessive 'couch potato' time.

15 I ask workload questions such as, 'Can this be delegated?', 'Can I do it now?' or 'Am I handling this twice?'.

16 I take periodic breaks, especially when I don't think I need them or when I am 'too busy'.

17 I balance work and home life well; I don't bring my work mind home, nor put in excessive overtime, and I am not a workaholic.

18 If I am doing work that can be done by another and which can and should be delegated, I do it with them—I do not do it alone (I teach by example).

19 If I am doing detail work, I strive to work myself out of whatever job I am currently doing.

20 I avoid the 'paralysis of perfectionism' and I am not a procrastinator.

21 I know how to say 'No!'.

22 I protect myself from things that rob me of my time.

23 I prefer doing important things to doing 'interesting' distractions.

Now, please read the list again, perhaps after a short break to integrate what you have seen, and fill out the following worksheet. For each numbered statement above, check whether it is a strength or area for improvement. Perhaps you want to check halfway between if neither extreme is accurate. The most important thing is to be honest—this is for your own information only!

I suggest you leave the 'description' column blank except for those things that are areas for improvement. Summarise the numbered statement that corresponds to this area in your own words, in ways that speak to you—don't use my words. It will be far easier to recognise these descriptions if they are sparse than if they fill the page.

When done, circle just one area that you would like to do something about right now. It might not be the biggest—it might be the one that speaks to you the most. Don't try too many areas at once, or you might give up and not do any. When you are all done with the first one, you can then do another, and so on. The problem for some people is that they have 'too many problems'.

Strengths/Areas for Improvement Worksheet

	Strength	Improvement	Description
1	( )	( )	_____
2	( )	( )	_____
3	( )	( )	_____
4	( )	( )	_____
5	( )	( )	_____
6	( )	( )	_____
7	( )	( )	_____
8	( )	( )	_____
9	( )	( )	_____
10	( )	( )	_____
11	( )	( )	_____
12	( )	( )	_____
13	( )	( )	_____
14	( )	( )	_____
15	( )	( )	_____
16	( )	( )	_____
17	( )	( )	_____
18	( )	( )	_____
19	( )	( )	_____
20	( )	( )	_____
21	( )	( )	_____
22	( )	( )	_____
23	( )	( )	_____

WHERE HAS THE TIME GONE?

The question of the year! (Or maybe, time management-wise, the 'question of the hour'.) Some time management practices from the old school suggest keeping a time log, doing it daily, doing it forever, making rigid notations...

And most people that have tried it have failed, not because it is inherently a bad idea, but because the way it is implemented is not realistic in today's world.

Even though we are in our own skin, we do not always have ownership of the things that happen to our time. And yet, we don't want to get obsessive over an analysis. Is there a practical approach?

Yes!

First, to prove to yourself that keeping some sort of written record for a short time is valuable, do this:

- Write down how often you think that the weather forecaster is right or wrong, expressed as a percentage. I realise this will be an emotional answer, not a logical one (if our picnic was rained out, we might be pretty mad about it).
- Then, over a span of a few days, compare the actual weather with the prediction.

What a surprise! Most people give the forecaster far less credit for accuracy than is due. Why is this? It is not because we were not there; it is because unexpected weather that affects us badly lasts in our memory longer than an accurate forecast that we don't care about.

For example, for over 30 years I lived in Northern New York State in the USA. One day, in the very late spring (almost summertime) we had 17 1/2 inches (over 44 cm) of snow when 'partly cloudy' weather was forecast. People travelled to work on their snow mobile machines! Of course, due to the hot weather, it all melted in two or three days. The point is that this happened in the early 1980s and I still remember it clearly today. I cannot tell you with any accuracy which day back then was sunny and clear!

And so it is with time. Big experiences, especially negative ones, make a profound impression on us, and we believe that these events take far more time than they do. In fact, other events such as repetitive 'time wasters' often take far more time than we imagine! It is amazing to note the number of hours often spent on impromptu 'pop-up' meetings, drop-in interruptions, or phone calls.

The purpose of any written record, or time log, is to note with accuracy where the time actually goes. The important thing is, once we have an understanding of where it goes, we do not need to continue logging it. Sometimes a task like logging seems very burdensome, especially if we think we have to do it forever.

On the other hand, we can put up with almost anything if we know we will do it for only a very short time.

So my suggestion is this:

1 Keep track of the way you spend your time on the following log, and only until you see a pattern. This may be as short as a day or two, and seldom longer than a week. Fill out only the 'comments and results' portion of the log, and leave preceding columns blank. Don't keep staring at your watch; keep track of 15–30 minute intervals by using a repetitive watch alarm. If away from your desk, summarise on a pocket dictating machine so it is fresh in your mind and record it later. Take only 10–15 seconds to record quickly so that your routine is not interrupted and you remain productive.

2 Compare what happens to your strengths/areas for improvements worksheet (see earlier), especially what you find surprising. Any interesting patterns?

3 Focus on changing some of the behaviours in that worksheet. For tough ones, try using the 'swish' technique (discussed below).

4 Repeat the logging process a little differently: establish a plan for the day in the 'action' and 'priority' columns, then cover those two columns over during the remainder of each day so that you record the 'comments and results' without viewing the planned actions and priorities.

5 See how well your achievements match your plans. This might not happen at the exact times you planned, and yet you are interested in how much, overall, you completed of what was planned. Again, continue this practice for one or two days or until you see a pattern, and for not longer than a week.

6 Complete the analysis checklist that follows.

Daily Time Log

DATE: _____   **GOALS:** _____

time	action	priority	comments and results
8:00			
8:30			
9:00			
9:30			
10:00			
10:30			
11:00			
11:30			
12:00			
12:30			
1:00			
1:30			
2:00			
2:30			
3:00			
3:30			
4:00			
4:30			
5:00			
5:30			
Later			

Analysis Checklist

1 Record time spent in the last column only, for a couple of days.

2 Compare to the Strengths/Areas for Improvements worksheet.

3 Work on changing behaviours, use 'swish' (explained shortly).

4 Repeat Step 1 and pre-plan; hide those columns and record.

5 Compare achievements to plans.

6 Did goal setting improve effectiveness?

_____

7 Were the goals realistic?

_____

8 Notice patterns: Do you constantly 'overbook'?

_____

9 When did you start your first goal? (Sometimes we have so many administrative tasks, we don't get to our useful work until later in the day!)

_____

10 To what extent was each objective achieved?

_____

11 Aside from meetings and lunch, what was your longest uninterrupted time? (Some work requires long blocks of time, and we may fragment our work too much.)

_____

12 Who, or what, was your most frequent interruption?

_____

13 What are its causes and possible controls?

_____

14 List necessary interruptions and possible controlling steps:

_____

_____

_____

15 List the five most time-consuming activities to be 'farmed out' or properly delegated:

1 _____

2 _____

3 _____

4 _____

5 _____

TIME WASTERS

After looking at your worksheet, logs and checklist, you may have noted some 'time robbers' that you would like to get rid of.

Some very big ones rate their own section in this book and will be discussed later. They include:

- imbalance between urgency and importance;
- delays due to stress and fatigue;
- lack of delegation or over-supervision;
- failure to communicate well;
- bad written communication;
- meetings;
- ineffective facilitation;
- inadequate problem solving;
- conflict;
- improper staffing, unmotivated staff; and
- mis-communication of requirements.

That is quite a list! Nevertheless, workshop groups frequently come up with more than a hundred time robbers.

One way to brainstorm the issues that are a problem for you would be to get your team together, and have each member write down all of the time robbers they can think of. Then, as a group, you can discuss them and rate them on size, frequency or irritation level. Some very common ones not treated as separate sections in this book and suggested solutions are :

- telephone tag (try leaving detailed information; ask for the best times to call back; be at your phone during certain published hours; call at times when they are likely to be at their desk and keep note of when);
- electronic mail (check e-mail only once per day; use screening systems; use the phone or personal visits instead, especially within the company);
- improper training (use just-in-time training for newly required project skills; place new recruits and trainees off the critical path);
- delays in availability of personnel (watch out for projects that are multi-threaded with others; check ahead of time to confirm that people really will be free when forecast; make sure their manager is a stakeholder in your project);
- project thrashing (ie spending time changing from one project to another) (minimise the number of simultaneous projects so that your wheels don't spin in the mud, getting you nowhere; guard and limit non-project time; partition your days or days within the week to have large blocks of time; avoid heavily incompatible projects);
- travel time or transit time between buildings (make good use of time on board aeroplanes; sort activities by building number, not task; use teleconferencing or video conferencing);
- conflicting or cross-purpose goals (make sure departmental goals are consistent with your project goals; form good rapport with functional managers, making them stakeholders; get clear project missions agreed to and endorsed up front);
- inadequate tools (use good automated tools to make scheduling and control less laborious; use adequate testing, workbenching and prototyping tools; plan logistical support and availability);
- over promising and under delivering, instead of under promising and over delivering (consult your time log; see if you constantly overbook yourself; note what you really accomplish; see if you are seeking approval or to be liked; notice if you feel you are overworked or always behind).

These are just some of the most 'popular' ones; there are many others. By looking closely at, and ranking, your biggest time wasters, you can become substantially more productive during your day.

4 Changing habits and NLP

Perhaps by now, you are aware (maybe acutely aware) of your own 'shortcomings'. Of course, they are not shortcomings at all, merely habits. These habits may be useful in other contexts, and just happen to be unproductive in projects. Maybe you really want to have more time for your family and just can't seem to get off the computer. Perhaps, when facing a very important task, you find yourself far too willing to do something that is an interesting distraction in order to procrastinate. Maybe you fly off the handle and get upset too easily when people do not perform as expected, or you don't get cooperation from other departments. Maybe, maybe, maybe…

There are a lot of good books that simply say, 'Do something else'. Well, if you could do something else, you would be doing it now, wouldn't you? Easier said than done!

There is a wonderful science called NLP, standing for Neuro-Linguistic Programming, which can be used very often to change these nuisance behaviours with a minimum of drudgery. A few words about how the science works:

How are some people so extraordinary at communicating and causing organisational change, while others remain ineffective? Until recently, science has been struggling with what these people do that makes the difference—with very limited results.

Limited, that is, until the development of NLP, a science developed in the early 1970s by Drs Richard Bandler and John Grinder. It is a systematic study of how we process information. Specifically, it is how we take facts through our five senses, and encode that data internally, then how we express it. Because it is based on how the brain actually works, it is the most defect-free communication science in existence.

Why has this not been done before? It is because many communications experts—indeed, most people who achieve excellence in any area—are not consciously aware of just how they do what they do, much less how to teach this to others.

To solve this dilemma, Bandler, Grinder and others began an exact study of several well-renowned experts in communication and behaviour change. These experts included Gregory Bateson, Milton Erickson, Fritz Perls and Virginia Satir. They found out how the experts achieved excellence; Bandler and Grinder then turned it into the science called NLP.

By learning NLP, you have new levels of awareness of human behaviours, from information provided through the five senses. By identifying specific language patterns (verbal and non-verbal) used by others, you can access the way other people process information in their minds. These formerly invisible 'maps of the world' are revealed to you via your new skills. By translating what you wish to say into the other's map, you become supremely able to communicate and to effect significant change. Not only are you effective, what you are saying is easier for the other to hear and understand—it just seems 'more comfortable'.

Since all good self-change work is nothing more than good communication with yourself, you also unlock boundless opportunities for your own improvement. What used to be limitations now are turned into abilities. Comfort, confidence, excellence and capability can be 'self-installed' to improve your interactions, management effectiveness, teaching, and presentation skills. It has been said that 'NLP teaches people to run their own brain instead of letting their brains run them'.

Old models attempt to 'change behaviour by changing behaviour'. The theory used to be that if you repeat a new behaviour often enough, over the years, you will eventually change old habits. Not only is this painstakingly slow, it often doesn't work or doesn't last. Subconscious desires often cause us to 'snap back' to old, ineffective ways of doing things. The reason these old methods don't work is because the brain doesn't operate that way! Therefore, we become equally ineffective at communicating with others or effecting organisational change.

WHY DOES NLP WORK?

The brain is like a computer, running 'control programs' in the same way that operating systems run on a personal computer. The brain's control program picks up 'applications' (habits and instinctive behaviours) and runs them, in the same way a personal computer runs applications like word processing or spreadsheets. It is not possible for the brain to remove applications, but it can always add to them. Better yet, it can use old programs as the basis for new ones. By the time we reach adulthood, we already have all the resources we need to accomplish change within ourselves. All it takes is translation from one set of 'applications' to another, the way one moves from one word processing product to another. This translation is effortless in contrast to the old attempts at changing behaviour the hard way.

Using NLP, a person interacts with the portion of the brain that makes the difference—the part that 'runs' the software—using the same methods as the mind itself. By teaching the brain how to select the 'applications', instead of how to change them, smooth and lasting change is the result.

Most NLP tools require yourself as the participant and another skilled person called a practitioner. There are a few techniques, however, that can be applied without the aid of another person. The first of these, called the swish technique, is described below.

THE NLP SWISH TECHNIQUE

This technique is useful for changing behaviours, or even attitudes, that do not work for you. It is useful in extremely specific contexts, for extremely specific behaviours or attitudes. It does not work well for very broad ranges of inappropriate behaviours, or in very broad contexts. However, in the project context, you should find it very useful. This technique works best for habits where you would wish to 'do this and not that'. So, if you find yourself as your own worst enemy, entertaining time robbers (and wishing you didn't) then this is the technique for you. It is not therapy; you cannot use it to quit smoking or for other major paradigms (in short, anything where you get too much 'good' out of the destructive behaviour). All of you must be interested in going for the change. So if you are in conflict about the new habit or behaviour, or think that the following technique is silly or stupid to do, then it will probably not be effective.

It can also be used to change counter-productive attitudes. Let me give you an example.

Shortly after I learned the technique in my beginning practitioner NLP class, I was standing in the hotel checkout line, having completed the overall training. The other participants and I were very, very ready to go home: we had been there for 16 days straight with virtually no breaks, and very enjoyable yet long days they were.

Something tickled my nose and I covered my mouth (properly, I thought) and sneezed. The woman in front of me in line said to her daughter, 'Oooooo…germs' and promptly whisked her daughter and herself out of the line into another line. It was also clear to me that she was not really talking to her daughter—she was speaking loudly enough for me to hear it, to try and make me feel bad or guilty.

Well, I was really upset—furious—livid. Please note: I made no plans to kill her, or hire a hit man, or anything else. I just noticed that this was the degree of my upset. I was quite sure that I did not want this to 'rent space in my head' for any prolonged period of time, and it was apparent it would not go away quickly by itself.

So, I used the swish technique while I stood in line—it took only about a minute— and the upset attitude that I had disappeared completely.

Of course I still knew what the woman was up to; I did not change the way the world worked, just my reaction to it. Before, my reaction was, 'How could she'? Afterwards it was, 'Well, that's her opinion'.

I am personally indebted to Robert Dilts of the NLP University, Santa Cruz, California, USA for creating this technique, and to Linda Sommer of the Eastern NLP Institute, New Hope, Pennsylvania, USA for sharing it with me during my initial NLP training and for giving permission for its use here.

Here is the technique.

THE SWISH PATTERN

1 *Think of the new behaviour.* Determine how, when or where you would like to behave differently or have a different attitude.

2 *Form the old picture.* Form a picture in your mind—bright, large, perhaps many feet or metres in size—of the way things are today, the behaviour or attitude that you would like to change. Be clear about the objects in the room or location, the people, the surroundings, the conversations, even the sounds and feelings you experienced then. Although you may have a mental idea of events and sounds, make sure it is a still picture rather than a motion picture or movie. Make sure you are associated with the picture; that is, you are looking through your own eyes at the world. Call this, the old picture. Let that picture disappear ('clear the screen') by setting it aside for the moment.

3 *Form the new picture.* Now form a new picture in your mind. This would be the way you would see yourself if you were behaving differently or had a different, new, productive attitude. This picture should be darker than the old picture, and the view should be dissociated; that is, you see all of you in the picture (the way a friend or camera would see you, or a video you watch of yourself). Now set that aside for a moment also.

4 *Form a composite.* Now take the large, bright, old picture of the way things used to be, as if through your own eyes, and put it in front of you. Place a very small, dark, new picture as if through another's eyes of the way you want things to be in any of the corners; I prefer lower left or right. Perhaps the old picture is huge, and the new picture is no bigger than a postage stamp. Even if it is tiny, you still have the memory of the details on it.

5 *Swish pattern.* In your mind, say: 'One, two, three, swish'. With the word swish suddenly make the tiny new picture very large and bright and the old picture small and dim. You can even imagine the new picture expanding suddenly and covering the old like wallpaper.

6 *Dissolve and repeat.* Now let both pictures dissolve or disappear and go back to step 4 to have them reform, and repeat the swish pattern in step 5. Repeat this pattern several times. If you are doing it properly, you should soon have difficulty in forming the original old picture properly. It might 'want' to jump to the new picture.

Congratulations! By following this technique, you should be able to notice a change in your behaviour.

Some of you may now get a sense, or feeling, of a change as well. Perhaps the old behaviour seems 'foreign'. Some people report that they have a memory of doing things the old way, yet it is as if that behaviour is something done by someone else. These feelings are normal.

The process works by changing size, brightness, and (eventually) association. The mind cannot tell the difference between something imagined with great accuracy and something actually done. Do you remember many years ago when the German Olympic team walked away with about seven gold medals? This is largely because they creatively visualised their top performance both in practice and at the competition itself.

This theory has been scientifically tested. A number of players were assembled for the American game of basketball. The idea was to measure the performance of basketball players throwing the ball from a marked distance into the overhead hoop and net, called foul shooting. The group was divided into three. The first group was asked to practise one hour a day for about a month. The second group was told to go home and do nothing. The third was told to practise foul shots only in their mind for 1 hour per day for the same period.

An amazing thing happened. The second group (the control group) that was told to go home and do nothing, got worse as you would expect. The first group that had actual practice got better—about 30% better. The third group, which practised only in their mind also got better—about 28% better—nearly as good as the group that did actually practise!

This shows the power of changing habits by using one's mind alone.

Some years ago, I was learning how to fly a helicopter. I already knew how to fly an aeroplane. I knew I had very little practice time in the helicopter, and I wanted to make every minute count. While no one can learn to fly an aircraft by reading a manual alone, nonetheless I studied the manual. I imagined myself in various flight regimes, manipulating the controls; I did this for several hours. On my first flight, within a very few minutes, I was flying, doing climbs and descents and turns, and even hovering the helicopter. I credit this not to extreme prowess, but to the visualisation that took place first.

Why do you visualise yourself associated in the old picture and dissociated in the new? Because your mind does not believe you are doing the activity the new way until the change takes place, and to make the setup otherwise would be to behave dishonestly with your mind. The 'safety mechanisms' in your mind automatically go off and kill the process.

Why not just shrink the new picture back to original size when repeating the process over and over? Because this essentially reverses the change you have just made. The swift swish action must go one way only; that is why you must interrupt the swish at that point and dissolve both pictures before reforming them and restarting.

If the process does not work well for you, examine the following:

- Were you 'honest' with your mind, by making pictures detailed and accurate, and did you really believe in the process?
- Did you invert the pictures you were associated or dissociated in, or get the sizes and brightnesses mixed up?
- Did you do the swish too fast or too slow for your own tempo?
- In the new picture, did you erroneously try to change the way others behaved? You should see only your own behaviour or attitudes changing, because you are the only one you can control.

I think you will find this a very useful technique!

5 Planning your day

Many people have asked me over the years how I keep track of so many projects and keep so many people happy, without going nuts, and still get a lot done! From time to time, I have shared some of my personal habits, expecting that they were peculiar to my personality or way of being.

However, in many seminars, I quickly learned that over half of the attendees could use many of the techniques I use to get through my day, in some cases letter for letter, and have great success with them! So I decided that they are not just peculiar to me, but are processes that others can learn.

A DAILY STRUCTURED TECHNIQUE

My daily technique works very well in extremely intense multi-project situations. Be sure to intermix a heavy dose of relationship, role orientation and family time along with this very detailed technical method. We will cover only the technical management of your office day here.

I shall start with the middle of one day and go to the middle of the next.

1   During the busy day, which is a mixture of multiple projects, non-project time and administrative duties, make no extensive attempt to re-plan your day or take copious notes of your activities. Short reminders are OK, perhaps on a pocket digital dictating machine.

2   At the end of the day, during the drive or ride home, dictate into a mini- or micro-cassette dictation machine (or a digital machine with larger memory) words or short phrases that remind you of the day's events. These can be questions, problems, tasks, reminders, solutions—small segments that tell you what happened. Stop and start the recorder so that all words will be close together on playback, even though there may be considerable delay between words during the drive. At first, the ideas will be fast and furious, and then may come in dribs and drabs with as much as a minute between them. For the average hectic day, a 20 minute drive should cover all of them.

3   Having safely stored the day's major events and 'catastrophes' on the machine, you can now actually bring something worthwhile through the door to your family—you! You won't be running the day's events through your head all night long, at least out of fear that you might forget them. Also, by not

focusing on problems constantly you may sometimes spawn solutions when you least expect them.

4   You should be able to get a pleasant night's sleep. Some people like to keep the pocket dictation machine near the bedside. You will probably find this not to be necessary unless you have not followed the preceding steps.

5   In the morning, on the drive or ride into work, rewind the tape and replay the words and phrases from yesterday afternoon. They will undoubtedly trigger new thoughts not available the day before. Stated problems from yesterday will evoke spontaneous solutions and ideas in your mind. At the end of the played back words, dictate these new solutions, ideas and tasks. Your tape now has yesterday's thoughts, immediately followed by today's ideas.

6   First thing in the morning, take some 'closed door' time to yourself. Take about 10–15 minutes of planning time, and play back the tape. Take written notes into your electronic scheduler or manual daily planner for that day and future days. From your time log discovery period (discussed earlier), see how much of your day is predictable or unpredictable. You may be able to schedule only 65% of your day-to-day known tasks with the rest left open because of unpredicted events, pop-up meetings, calls, or simply being quickly responsive in the name of good customer service.

7   Once a day, briefly re-evaluate how the workload within that week is going. Do major planning once a week and minor alterations only on a daily basis. Once a week, look at the month; once a month, look at the quarter and so on. 'Load balance' your days and weeks this way.

8   With the exception of the 'slack' time built into your schedule, try this awful-sounding rule: *don't do anything new today*. This really means that you have taken a lot of time to be prevention-based and to plan things for the day and week; seldom can you spontaneously react and do better planning on the fly than you did in a structured manner. This does not mean be rigid; there are times when the plan has to be set aside for unusual emergencies. And that is the point—they should be truly unusual. Which is better: attempting to deliver everything today and failing to do it for a week, or always getting to it tomorrow, when you said you would? Think about it!

9   To avoid the fear of 'underbooking' yourself based on your computations of what you know you can do, realise this: if you finish your work early, you can just turn the page in your daily planner or hit the page down key on the computer and look at tomorrow's work! What if, day after day, tons of incomplete items are constantly spilling over from today to tomorrow to the next day? Soon you have a growing mound of backlog that no-one can fathom. There is something very destructive for your emotions and self-empowerment about never being finished and falling further and further behind. It is a very negative self-statement to be constantly faced with reminders that 'you never did what you said you would do'.

Now, none of these planning techniques are intended to substitute for rational thought, a balanced life or common sense. They are tools to get you through the toughest of times. If you find some of them don't work for you, change them! For example, some people are evening people rather than 'morning' people; they prefer to plan at the end of the day rather than the beginning. So, modify these techniques to meet your own needs!

GENERAL DAILY PLANNING

Planning a project overall is an important event. Equally important, however, is the kind of planning needed to handle multiple projects and how they interleave with one another, and even with non-project time. General daily planning is the way in which you build a 'mini project plan' for the interplay among multiple projects and non-project time.

You can be a project manager and a team member at the same time, of course, because you can manage one project while being a 'doer' on another. In today's world, seldom do we have the clear cut advantage of being a project manager or team member for one project only. Even as a project manager, we do not often have the luxury of being in charge of a multi-person project that is so large that our only task is that of project manager and not 'doer'. Depending on the project size, many things can happen:

- You could be the project manager of a very large project, perhaps planning the activities of other project managers on smaller segments or phases, and be doing nothing else.
- You could be managing a modest project (6–18 months, 6–10 people) with your main job being project management only; however, you are also a team member on one or more other projects and may have minor tasks on your main project.
- You could be in a small, one or two person project where you must be not only the project manager, but also a highly productive team member. Certainly this is the case if you are in a one person project, where you are the 'chief cook and bottle washer'.
- In addition to two or three projects of various sizes in which you both manage and participate in the task work, you have a number of other non-project activities that you must lead or participate in. These could include leading or receiving training, undertaking administrative tasks, or other functions.

For these reasons, we need a model similar to project planning, yet different in scope.

I call this: Manage Your GORATE. The acronym GORATE stands for:

- Goals
- Opportunities
- Resources
- Activities
- Timetable
- Evaluation

We use the word 'opportunities' instead of those we normally might use, eg 'problems' or 'roadblocks'. Some people call them 'challenges'. The important thing is to think of them in positive terms.

I suggest coupling this model with the daily structured technique in the preceding section. When you have enumerated certain tasks for the day, you can use this method for some of the larger ones. Specifically, if the task is a 'quickie' like a telephone call or quick errand, then no task planning may be needed. This GORATE method is handy for those 'pieces' of one half hour to two hours in length for example.

First, for each mini-task that qualifies, set your goals or what you want to achieve. Then, identify the challenges, problems, roadblocks or opportunities that perhaps stand in your way so you have a mental task plan. Next, identify who will do it and whatever other supplier or financial resources are needed. Following this, list the activities in the mini-task plan that need to be programmed to accomplish the objective. Identify the timetable by which the goals need to be done and their mini-tasks. Finally, define an evaluation process to confirm that the actions actually achieved the goal and overcame any symptoms and problems.

Sometimes, this general planning model needs to be used to treat the interplay among projects, and not just the mini-tasks of the day. There may also need to be a strategy for handling non-project time while still giving good customer service to 'pop-up' requests. This model can be used whenever the task is not trivial. It can be as quick as a 10-second mental run-through to assure you are well organised, or even a minute or two for larger tasks. Try it!

By managing your own handling of time well, and having a model to stratify and synchronise colliding priorities, you will be a model of performance to your people as a project manager. Note that this technique is equally important for project team members.

6   Dynamics of change

To be a great model for others in today's world, it is simply essential that you understand the dynamics of change.

The only thing constant about today's competitive marketplace is that it is changing. Some people estimate that in the span of just one decade, 75% of the world's work force will have retrained. Companies that functioned well for so many years now have to withstand dramatic upheaval. Just look at technology, the Internet, and South East Asia markets as examples. In our lifetimes, the Soviet Union is no more, the Berlin Wall has fallen, Hong Kong has reverted to Chinese rule, and leaders in shipping and trading have swung from one country to another. As Tom Peters once said, 'The whole economic thing is up for grabs'.

When implementing a quality program, the standards and procedures are constantly in flux to meet the needs of ever changing processes. Continuous improvement forces continuous change, and just when a product is stable and nearly the best, along comes the need for an all-new product, restarting the continuous improvement cycle all over again. Project personnel, by the very definition of what constitutes a project, are dealing with all-new, changed territory in each new project.

CHANGE IS LIKE BETRAYAL

If you look closely, many of us would rather be 'comfortably miserable'. Although we may not admit it, there is a certain stability in sameness. Yes, the job may be boring, or yes, we are doing the same old thing over and over again, yet at least we know what is expected. There is more nervousness of the unknown, even though the leap to the unknown may be positive progress. The 'betrayal' is the rocking of our stability.

Imagine a trapeze artist in a circus. Even with talent and training, there is a period of time when the performer is in the air, having swung from one bar to another. This is 'hanging out in the space', trusting that the other bar will be in the right position at the right time. There is a certain amount of uncertainty, overcome only with knowledge, timing and capability.

Have you ever jumped up and down on a trampoline? Have you ever gone through a period of weightlessness like the trapeze artist, for any reason? For many of us, it gives us 'butterflies' in our stomach, and is more than a little bit uncomfortable. For some of us, we get the same sensation looking out over the edge of a very tall building. We are secure, yet it feels very strange.

Sometimes we have only the knowledge that our project management techniques or quality program will work, and yet no absolute proof. We are on uncharted territory, hanging out in the spaces, and it is uncomfortable. We don't have the security of the 'same old' thing. I want to acknowledge the difficulty and share with you that this tension and change are necessary and are the lifeblood of all successful projects. We cannot be rigid and be successful; as much as we plan, we must be ready for dynamic, unexpected change.

CHANGE TAKES TIME

The full adaptation to change usually takes people a certain amount of time. Lyle Yorks and David Whitsett* did a study over a 20-year period, and found that some people were very adaptive to change and others were not. Some were so adaptive that they were likely to be the ones creating change. Others were so fixed that they would either not adapt, would 'shoot' the change agent, or leave the company.

This research shows that there are five types of people in terms of adaptability to change. Organisations usually have a blending of each of these types. The smallest populations are the ones on either extreme, with the largest population usually in the middle. Here are the types:

- Innovators
- Early adaptors
- Conforming adaptors (biggest group)
- Late adaptors
- *Boiled frogs*

Innovators are change agents, who most likely both adapt early and create the change, or implement new procedures, in the first place. Visible or invisible, these people often lead dynamic change in the organisation, and are important players in projects, new products and any quality movement.

Early adaptors, although somewhat less creative, are among the first to try out the new process and are very open to checking out new things, even if they did not 'make' them. These are the people who eagerly 'beta test' new products or software. They are willing to withstand some early glitches in order to be in the forefront of technology.

---

* L. Yorks & D.A. Whitsett 'Scenarios of Change' Praeger Publishers pp 48–49 & 203–205 (New York, NY, 1989)

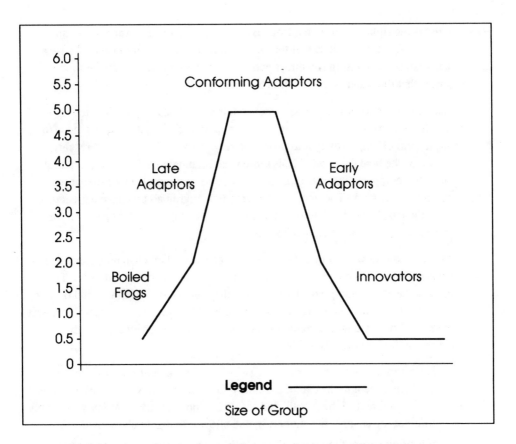

Conforming adaptors is perhaps the largest group of people in any organisation. Change is somewhat uncomfortable for them, and it takes time. Nevertheless, after a certain period, they are willing to try the new procedure, and will warm to it with experience. Sometimes this time delay is called 'culture change'.

Late adaptors are perhaps as late at change as the early adaptors are early! While they may complain more, and perhaps explicitly resist, they will come along in time. A late adaptor will be slower than a conforming adaptor, yet would rather change eventually than leave the company.

That leaves our last category—the 'boiled frogs'. This metaphor has some meaning to those who enjoy frogs' legs as a delicacy.

Anyone who has cooked a frog for dinner knows that if you throw a live frog into boiling water, it jumps out. After all, frogs are not stupid! The same analogy applies to the people who are these latest of adaptors of all. If you 'throw' these folk into a new quality program, project output or procedure, they 'jump out' by either leaving the company, killing the procedure or both.

What is the right way to boil a frog? By putting the frog into warm water and then turning on the heat so that the water temperature rises gradually. The frog has relatively thick skin (no direct pun or analogy intended), so by the time it senses that the water is too hot, it is too late.

Taking this humorous (or perhaps, not so humorous) analogy further, the right way to 'boil' your company 'frogs' who are extremely resistant to change is to implement change slowly and progressively. This is also what the research shows: by the time these individuals sense what is going on, it is too late; practically the entire company has changed, and complaints or attempts to kill the process will no longer work. The new activities are now ingrained and have a great deal of resilience. The individual still may not like the change, and may search for another job and leave the organisation.

The research shows that in order to be most effective, key champions and change agents need to create a groundswell, or critical mass, of committed allies. This needs to permeate and gradually take over the organisation over a period of time. Consistent with this, note that any new quality initiative, or new project's product or service, or any new procedure or standard, constitutes change. Accordingly, the research also notes the following:

- Do not give fancy new names, buzzwords or the like to new programs or products except to the extent necessary. Otherwise, many will think that this is the 'program of the month' and say, 'This too shall pass'. Many will simply wait out the change, not support it, and allow it to die an untimely death.

- It is often best not to give too much public, showy recognition to the key change champion, or 'shining star' responsible for the change, as this makes him or her an easy target for boiled frogs.

- Try to find ways of integrating the change into the ways you are already doing business. Perhaps existing words or terms could be used for new actions. Flashy new programs are easy targets and are usually not best either; see if they can be promoted as a modest alteration to an existing program.

A profound, real illustration of all these points (flashy program, too fast, new words, shining star) occurred in one of the food divisions of a large midwest USA conglomerate. A new, highly successful TQM (total quality management) program was launched and 'successfully' implemented very rapidly. It was an all-new program, with new buzzwords, and was very flashy. There were many celebrations, and tremendous visibility was given to the chief architect, the plant manager. In fact, this caught the attention of the corporate office on the East Coast, and the manager was promoted to a position there and transferred out east.

The boiled frogs were just waiting. Shortly after he left, they systematically destroyed and disassembled the initiative, returning the plant to the methods and techniques in use before the change! This true story gives us fair warning.

There are occasional exceptions. Everything mentioned above essentially says to match people where they are. In an extraordinary example, one organisation transformed almost overnight.

In the Canadian Maritime Provinces, a government ferry service was privatised, and an individual was called back out of retirement to run the new ferry service. He was very knowledgeable in TQM techniques, which was certainly not the way people were used to doing business on the ferry.

On a Friday afternoon, he rallied the workers and sailors around. He had heard that many of these programs take years to implement, and, according to his doctor, he didn't have that kind of time left. So he told the workers that instead they would start practising TQM on Monday. He shared information about the program, and told them where they could get more information and references. He also said that anyone was free not to participate—provided they came up front and picked up a self-selected 'pink' slip (meaning that they were fired). By the way, some did just that. Guess what: on Monday, the culture had changed completely, and everyone was practising the principles!

So what is culture change? It is nothing other than the majority of the individuals in the organisation practising the new way of doing business. The key word is *individuals*. A company is not some huge mass with great inertia; it is nothing other than the sum of a number of individuals. It is not any harder for any one person to change than for all individuals to change, because everyone is working independently. Perhaps it can be said that culture change is *each one* of the individuals making the needed change independently.

You might argue that the transition was fear-based, contrary to Deming's principles (see Chapter 2). So why did this work? The manager was indeed an empowering manager. It is not an unusual sea-faring style to rule by hierarchy, discipline and even fear. The manager knew that people understood direct orders with the overtone of consequence, because that is what they were used to. In other words, he was matching their experience. Although it is true that you cannot solve a problem using the same kind of thinking that created it, you may have to use the current culture's styles and methods to effect change into the new culture.

So that is the key: move people from where they are, to where they need to be. Do not simply move them where they need to be, without matching and leading them from where they are.

PREPARE PEOPLE

People have to go through less tumult if they can be prepared for the change at hand.

If people are used to a certain way of doing things, and then suddenly are thrust into a change, there is sure to be a reaction. In some cases, the reaction is a genuine, bona fide comment about how the new product, process or initiative should have been designed. In most cases, however, it is just 'venting' of frustration, using detailed comments as an excuse.

We so often design a new process or product, work in a team to tune it and get it all ready and in final form, and then 'spring' it on a very unwilling audience. Then, we seem so surprised at people's negative reaction to all of our hard work. We seem unappreciated. And yet, we brought this on ourselves.

Suppose we exhibited the incomplete process to future users even before it was done? Of course it would not be ready; people understand that. However, people will then have time to gradually adapt to the new techniques. Better yet, their reactions will have valid process comments mixed in—a great way of tuning the product and making mid-course corrections to ensure more defect-free results. In essence, we have shortened the time for change by preparing people in advance.

PAST KNOWLEDGE BIASES RESULTS

Repeatedly, we see how the lessons of the past can 'pollute' the experiences of the present. This can prevent people from achieving the added productivity of the use of the new product, service, or procedure right away. When people are properly prepared, given time and allowed the disruption of the change, they eventually will speed up using the new procedure.

This is why the best time to measure performance with the procedure is not right away: it is after the process has been in use for a while. You may have heard the well-known story of the woman cutting the end off the joint of meat before putting it into the roaster for the oven. When asked why, she didn't know other than that was how she was taught. Her mother did not know either, but her grandmother knew: the grandmother's roaster pan had an odd shape, and without cutting the end off the meat, it would not fit into the roaster! Of course, with the new roaster, this was not a problem, yet the habit remained long after the reason for the habit disappeared.

You might want to note how you limit yourself, based on past experience, rather than current paradigms.

SET SIGHTS HIGHER PROGRESSIVELY

For all the reasons above (betrayal, time, preparation, bias) it is hard for people to meet performance standards initially. No person ever mastered the sport of high jumping by setting the bar above their head and trying to jump over it—they would hit their head! They start with the bar low, and raise it by a small increment each time and continue the practice, until they eventually reach that great height.

And so it is with the standards expected of new, changed processes. People using the product or process, or even developing it as a team member, should start by setting standards at the current level of performance. Then, the process for development or usage should be improved, resulting in a new, higher standard being met. Finally, the standard is moved up to the new current level of performance. For this reason, standards and procedures are never fixed in high quality operations.

Notice how people set their own standards, and how the current performance standard is led by current performance, and not vice versa. This is very important: standards are not something to 'shoot for': they are 100% achievable by everyone who is properly initiated and trained.

SUMMARY

Important lessons on the introduction of organisational change

One must:

- prepare others carefully for change;
- defuse the political impact of change;
- defuse the cultural impact of change;
- defuse the emotional impact of change;
- provide informational alternatives during change;
- measure and make people aware of the increases in the quality, quantity and flexibility created by change;
- provide rewards for change;
- employ an appropriate time line for change; and
- keep supervisors and subordinates involved in the change.

Important skill development

Anticipate problems of change by:

- talking with others;
- making a plan;
- modifying the plan;
- seeking outside help; and
- evaluating performance.

Goals of change

Increases in:

- quality, quantity and flexibility of group performance;
- increased pride in work; and
- increased understanding of self and technology.

7 Your real, ideal and expected self

In addition to handling time, planning, and change, we now need to pay attention to an important part of integrity—are you 'walking the talk?'

WALKING THE TALK

It is true that this section shows how you communicate with others, and most of that work is contained in Section 3, *Getting others' houses in order*. So why do we look at this communication piece in this chapter, which deals with the self?

Simple! You, yourself, want to know whether *all* of you shows through in your conversations. I believe this is best—even if you don't like all the parts of you! The more of you that is real, and shows through your conversations, the better. Why? Because people quickly learn to follow the internal message (the 'body language' message, or 'meta' message, or the actual behaviours) rather than the spoken words alone. Perhaps 80% of your communication is this 'meta' message (along with your actions), with only 20% spoken. Some of what we get this way is unconscious, perhaps, yet it is still very powerful.

Others may say that once you spend a great deal of time with a person, you get to know what makes them tick, and then you can understand them. That, of course, is true. What most folks don't realise is the powerful impression that is often formed on first meeting. We want to be sure that all of who we are, being real, is communicated substantially in a very short time. Some applications for making sure your personality is well understood in just a short time include:

- first meetings with suppliers or customers;
- first meetings with the project team;
- first meetings with team member's management;
- executive presentations; and
- teaching situations.

Why is being *real* so important?

Whether you are a project manager or a team member, people know and trust you by your actions and your words. If there is a mismatch between what you say and what you do, many people immediately feel it in their 'gut'. The words make sense, yet they are puzzled—how come it feels wrong? Even if they act on the words, they find themselves betrayed later because true belief systems eventually come out as actions.

So, the desired outcome is to ensure that the message sent equals the message received, and for the actions to match.

Life isn't so easy. For many of us, some of what we portray is real, some is our own projection (ideal) and the rest is the listener's projection (expected).

Concepts and definitions

- *Real self:* who you think you are, that you can effectively communicate to others;
- *Ideal self:* who you think you are, that others do not discern from your communication;
- *Expected self:* who others think you are, but you do not base on your communication.

Skills (to be gained from the practice exercise below)

- *Cueing skills:* assertiveness, story telling, use of examples;
- *Listening skills:* self, object differentiation;
- *Negotiating skills:* meta-communication.

Goals

- to get others to expect from you what you expect from yourself;
- to know how others see you;
- to develop strategies and techniques for self-presentation.

Exercise:
Real, Ideal and Expected Self

To analyse how well you do in this area, I recommend that you choose two business partners who you do not know very well (who will know you solely as a result of your communication). Follow the steps below.

1 Working by yourselves, write up to 10 'self statements' in the 'My Self Statements' area of the worksheet below. Use very short, one- or two-word phrases that describe who you are, and be non-judgemental. For best results, be honest and accurate—only you will see this sheet. Your self statements may be like these: polite, honest, caring, selfish, obstinate, bullish, aggressive, passionate, capable...

2 Number yourselves one, two and three and get two blank sheets of paper each. Label each sheet with the names of the other two people. Now each person should have one name per sheet, naming the other two participants.

3 Person one (you) will go first. Set the worksheets and papers aside, and ask person two or three to pick a controversial, emotional, or passionate topic *of their choosing*, not yours. Take five minutes and address the topic to the two listeners. No writing during listening, please.

4 Now, persons two and three take the blank sheets with person one's name on them (not the worksheet) and, based on this conversation alone, attempt to determine what are the self statements of person one. Don't dwell on this; first impressions are important. Remember, short one- or two-word phrases only. It can be difficult to compare long sentences with long sentence to determine matches (which will happen later). Meanwhile, person one rests.

5 Now, rotate positions so that everyone gets a turn. Person two will speak, persons one and three will listen, then record on the sheet with person two's name. Finally, person three speaks and the process repeats.

6 After everyone has had a turn, exchange sheets with names on them in such a way that everyone has their own named sheet. Examine your worksheet with your self statements on it. All of you should work privately on this at the same time.

7   a) If any phrases on either or both papers match your 'my self statements', copy them down into the 'real self statements' portion of the worksheet and check them off the papers. This is who you think you are and that others apparently get from your conversation.

b) Then copy all the leftover, unused 'my self statements' into the 'ideal self statements' section of the worksheet. This is who you think you are, that only you are aware of (at least from the conversation).

c) Finally, copy all of the leftover, unused phrases from both sheets into the 'expected self statements' area of your worksheet. This is what others think of you, that you don't know about yourself.

8   Thank your partners. Seldom will you have this thorough an opportunity for introspection!

Knowing yourself worksheet

My Self Statements

1 _____

2 _____

3 _____

4 _____

5 _____

6 _____

7 _____

8 _____

9 _____

10 _____

Real Self Statements

1 _____

2 _____

3 _____

4 _____

5 _____

Ideal Self Statements

1 _____

2 _____

3 _____

4 _____

5 _____

Expected Self Statements

1 _____

2 _____

3 _____

4 _____

5 _____

6 _____

7 _____

8 _____

9 _____

10 _____

Here is what it says:

The more real-self statements, the better. Great! That is your goal. (Remember, the fact that not everything has been placed here does not mean you are false or dishonest. It simply means that the way you communicate does not do full service to your character.)

'Ideal' means ideal in the logical sense—it does not mean good or bad, but your own ideal of what you are, not communicated to others. If you have been trying to hide what you think is a bad facet of yourself, then you've succeeded (only to surprise your team later, so I don't recommend it). If you have qualities that you are proud of, however, they don't seem to come across in this short conversation. Work on showing that part of your character more fluently through language, spoken and unspoken.

'Expected' means expected by others, not found by you. This could be a good quality and you are selling yourself short. (In other words, it is part of a 'my self statement' and you did not even know it.) It could also be an irritating area you did not even know you had. It is important to do personal work on that part of your personality if that is your goal (note—your goal is not to hide it). It could also be strictly the hallucination of either or both of the listeners and might have nothing to do with you—it might be their own projections! However, if both listeners said the same thing, then it is less likely to be a bad guess; consider it.

By repeating this exercise from time to time, you will constantly improve your presentation and awareness and congruity, as more and more of the phrases turn up in the 'real self' category. Good luck!

8 Handling stress

If improperly handled, projects—even life—can be stressful. Wayne Dyer once said, 'There is no stress in the world—there are only people thinking stressful thoughts'. He is correct on this point. The evidence is that two people can be placed in the same 'stressful' situation; one can become stressed and the other not be disturbed by it at all. Nonetheless, there are types of events and activities that seem to lead more people to choose stressful thoughts. By comparison, there are events and activities that cause fewer people to become stressed. So you need to understand that the decision (whether conscious or unconscious) to choose a stressful thought is yours, and that situations can have a tendency to 'help' you to make that choice. The good news is that it is up to you, and there are techniques to assist.

As I said in the preface, I learned many project techniques the hard way—trial and error. One of the things I stumbled on quite early is a way of going beyond coping with stress, to handling it well, to not even having stress. At the peak of my project career, with six simultaneous projects running plus departmental responsibilities, one of the administrative assistants wanted to know how I did it. She commented that she and others had one or two projects, and were 'going nuts'; how could I remain calm in the face of many more projects? This section tells you how.

I believe that stress is primarily caused by two factors:

- the decision that you have not done the best you can; or
- the attempt to take control of something that is, or should be, out of your control.

If you trace back why you are stressed, you will probably find that it is due to one of these factors. Unless you deal with them, your effectiveness as a project manager or team member will be quite limited.

In this book, we have emphasised the importance of prevention. We have techniques for preventing the onset of stressful events in the first place, which is the more desirable approach. We will share ways of correcting stress once it has occurred, which is also important.

STRESS PREVENTION TECHNIQUES

The first cause, thinking that you are not doing the best job you can, has been addressed in our topic on 'A daily structured technique' (Chapter 5). People become stressed by constantly over-promising and under-delivering. When your task list gets bigger and bigger, with no end in sight, or you know that you rushed a job and didn't do it with pride and with care, the problems that can result cause a good deal of stress. The *structured technique* helps, because of its thorough yet pragmatic planning approach. Even if you do not accomplish all you would like, you get the feeling that you did an excellent job of organising all that you did. Because of the planning, you also get the feeling that no one could have been more productive or have done the right things in a better order than you did. So, it is not necessary to complete all your tasks to relieve stress, just to believe that you did the best you could. If you are running around crazy, simply reacting to emergencies, you know you could have done a better job!

There is another prevention-based technique—that of not trying to take control of something that is, or should be, out of your control.

Notice this statement has two parts: what *is* out of your control, and what *should be* out of your control.

Let us look at the *is* part. Many of us know that our success may be very limited when we try to change other people or departments, or try to force other managers to come around to our way of thinking, or force others to change schedules and budgets. We may also get frustrated. While it is important to do 'missionary' work and be good salespeople, having a stake in the outcome of changing other people can often leave you very stressed indeed. The best thing to do, as this section of the book is called, is to get your own house in order first, and let that be an example to others. I suggest you avoid hoping too much that you can absolutely change others. So, my suggestions in this area are easy (easy to say, harder to do)!

Now for the next part—the *should be* (out of your control) part. As a project manager, you may have theoretical control over what others (team members, for example) are supposed to do. Yet you still get overloaded, stressed, pushed and pulled, even when you hold all the cards. What is happening?

Should be means that just because you are in control of ways of doing things, it does not mean that it is proper that you take control. Doing so leads to stress.

To be specific, this means that if you are doing the work that others can be doing, delegating improperly, micro-managing or not encouraging new levels of initiative, then you can get very overloaded and stressed.

When looking at where your time goes as a manager, you notice you have only so much, and it is already apportioned in certain ways.

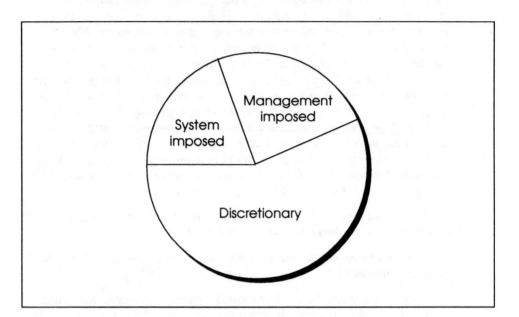

'System imposed' time is imposed by the organisation as a whole. It can include administrative tasks, training and some meetings. 'Management imposed' time is requested of you by your management, such as tasks or other projects required to make your department run smoothly. If you wish to keep your job, then neither of these two can be considered discretionary.

That leaves the remaining piece of the pie, well under 100% (in some cases perhaps under 50%). This is the portion of your time that is up to you, your 'discretionary' time. Or is it? That is the problem.

Depending upon the *level of initiative* shown by your people, you may be taking on too many pieces of their work or handling problems that actually, they can solve. Some examples:

One of your team members comes to you and says, 'We have a problem. It looks like…'. The problem is the word we! Of course you have the ability to take it on or not. However, you also realise your team member may be immobilised until you help him or her solve it. Not wanting your person to be idle, you assist them. You may want to tend to it right away, because they are waiting for you. Not only that, since it often takes longer to help them solve their own problem than just solving it yourself, you may be tempted to 'fix' it for them. Worse, you get a bolster to your ego by spending so little time to get the job done. You have the satisfaction of doing 'real' work, of helping others, and doing it in a fraction of the time they would have taken. Seems logical and makes sense, right?

Wrong!

You have just taught the team member to depend on you, and perhaps to be idle the entire period while they wait for your solution. It does not matter how little time it takes to fix it—the delay encountered by the team member may be considerable, having high cost to the project. They have successfully thrown the monkey on your back.

Here is another example: you decide that, for project 'control' purposes, you will 'micro-manage' your team, heavily supervising every activity. You require that they get your written approval before doing certain actions. Nothing goes on without your knowledge. Good management, right?

Wrong!

If you are an executive, you have an average of 17 hours of meetings a week, according to surveys; maybe somewhat less in the case of a manager. In any event, your team member may have to wait hours or days just for your two minute job of approving their work. They are idle once again, and the monkey has been on your back the whole time.

Perhaps, in another case, you feel that you are unloading the responsibility back when your team member comes to you with a problem, and you want to use your time efficiently and document it. You say, 'Interesting problem. Research it and give me an e-mail on that'.

Let's look. Initially, the monkey is on your team member's back. What is the very first thing they are going to do? Drop everything, gather the data for the problem, and send off the e-mail. Now the monkey is back on your back to solve it.

Even if you had 100% discretionary time and no system- or manager-imposed time, your time would disappear very quickly. Let's say you have 10 team members on your project. If each of them occupied only 10% of your day with their problems, your day would be gone! And they have only spent 10% of their day working with you on it! Not only that, if they successfully delegated the problem 'upward', you may be doing the 10% and they may be doing zero! The problem gets worse when you realise that your discretionary time is far less than 100% of the pie. Remember, it is in this discretionary time that you work on far more than the issues of your team members. This is the time slice in which you must also manage your project, handle non-project things, and perhaps do detailed project tasks. Perhaps even 5% of each team member's time would overload you!

Perhaps you get so busy that you eagerly come in during the weekend to catch up on some much needed priorities. You then learn that your team members have taken the weekend off to go sightseeing (after all, they successfully delegated their problems upward to you)! Who is working for whom?

To stay sane you simply have to change this paradigm. I have a pair of *golden rules* that I use for management:

- seldom, if ever, do anything alone; and
- work yourself out of whatever job you are in.

Simple, but effective.

In addition, I suggest you build a grid of team member names on one axis of a matrix, and a 'degree of initiative' on the other axis, and rate your people:

Name	Degree of Initiative				
	1	2	3	4	5
Name 1	✗				
Name 2			✗		
Name 3				✗	
Name 4		✗			

Enter the following scores for the degree of initiative, which is how self-empowered your people are on the team:

1   This person *waits* to be told what to do. When they finish a task, they notify no-one, and you have to notice that they are done and assign another. This is the lowest degree of initiative. If the person has any issues or problems, they simply stop and notify no-one.

2   This person *asks* what to do next. Although there is still no automatic initiative, at least you do not have to find out if they are idle. However, they will wait for you to be available for the next assignment. This person also asks for the solutions to problems that they have.

3   This person *recommends* what they feel they should do next. However, they still require your permission to proceed, or at least your blessing. The good trait here is that you do not have to do all the creative 'what is the next task' work for them. This person also recommends the solution to a problem, and needs to have you work on it with them.

Caution: even if your team member has an initiative level of four or five (see below), any hierarchical management style that requires your 'signoff' before proceeding automatically throws them back to level three. Therefore, you could be stopping their initiative at this point and making the problem yours!

4   This person *acts* on their own and, out of fear that they may have done the wrong thing, disruptively reports immediately to you about the actions they have taken. This is a high degree of initiative, with much disturbance associated with it. You are asked to do a 'post mortem' evaluation of whether they made the right decision, taking decision time of your own. They solve problems, and come to you to validate their solutions.

5   This person *acts* on their own as well, and reports what they have decided in the normal course of events, such as at the weekly status meeting. They also solve problems and do not require you to validate their solutions, simply reporting results in the ordinary flow of business. This is the highest degree of initiative.

Based on these definitions, place a check mark in the box that corresponds to your knowledge of their degree of initiative. The rule is that on each meeting, in each interaction, you should aim to slowly move that person from their current degree of initiative to the next higher one. You do not jump a 'one' to a 'five' overnight. You slowly convert a waiter into an asker, an asker into a recommender, and so forth. Notice this may mean taking longer to solve a problem. Instead of giving them the answer that you happen to know in just a few seconds, you take a little longer. You might ask them how and where would they locate the resources to solve their problem. You teach them what they need to know to be resourceful on their own. Of course it takes a little longer at first: because it is prevention based! All prevention-based approaches appear to add time to the project, as we saw in Chapter 2.

Remember, if you solve a team member's problem, no matter how quickly, they know you are the 'answer person' and you must do that for them over and over again. Worse than this, they wait for your availability for the answer, which could be hours for a one minute solution, delaying the entire project.

There is a saying that goes, 'Give a person a fish, and they eat for a day. Teach a person to fish, and they eat for a lifetime'.

To aid in this initiative-building process, use the two golden rules I mentioned earlier. Showing and demonstrating while solving not only teaches a person how to fish, it also unburdens you from your present job of constantly bailing out your people, and returns discretionary time to you.

I also suggest that you decide together when you determine what the next move is and who will make it. It should never be allowed to become vague or indefinite. All work in this area, including problem solving, should be done face-to-face or by telephone, and never by mail (including fax or e-mail). Otherwise, the next move could become yours and the monkey could wind up on your back again.

By restoring your discretionary time you will have more time to plan projects correctly and to complete otherwise leftover tasks. You will have a new sense of regaining control over your life.

CORRECTION TECHNIQUES

Try as we will, we do not always succeed at delegating properly. We put too much on our plates, or get our noses in other people's business. We are human, and we are tempted, and as a result, forgo the techniques from time to time, and Bang! there we are, stressed out still, from time to time. It is important to have some methods for removing the stress that creeps in due to our lack of vigilance.

There are two techniques shown here—a thorough, longer technique best done at home, and a shorter one for emergencies, which can be done in the office.

Thorough method

The first technique—the thorough one—is best done at home. It is powerful, and the effects are cumulative. It is the *progressive relaxation response and visualisation* technique. It is based on the knowledge that when the mind is tense or stressed, the body becomes that way too. Also, powerful visualisation of an alternative can release the mind. Science, including medical science, has embraced this technique as valid and useful for a variety of reasons.

To summarise the technique generally:

1   Once a day, or at least several times a week, at the same time of day (usually before retiring or shortly after arising) do this process. It takes 10–15 minutes.
2   Sit erect, and progressively relax individual muscles from head to foot.
3   Visualise a box or treasure chest that receives named stressful events that is then locked and reeled out of sight.
4   Re-awaken muscles from foot to head individually.

Here it is in more detail:

Step 1

It is important to do this as a regular practice because of its cumulative effects. If you rush off to work and don't think you have time, take note: the time you save by not being stressed out is far greater than the time you spend on this practice on a daily basis.

It does not matter whether you do this in the morning or evening. You should not be too tired when doing it. It is important to be sitting erect, so your body does not associate the position with sleep.

Step 2

The progressive relaxation of muscles relaxes the mind. When the mind is tense, the body is tense, and vice versa; when you relax the body, then the mind relaxes too. The body affects the mind, and the mind affects the body.

Identify muscles individually to insure thoroughness. It is too easy to gloss over the relaxation if you think only of whole areas. Some people prefer to flex the muscles just prior to relaxation, which helps identify the tension. You will know if a muscle is already tense because tensing it makes no difference! Otherwise, you might think it is already released and not know. In your mind, identify individual muscles in the scalp, forehead, face, neck, shoulders, and so on.

Keep only enough tension to keep your head erect, and plan a seated posture that is comfortable. Position yourself in such a way that it will not be necessary to move at all during the process. For you, this probably means feet flat on the floor, legs uncrossed, and arms comfortable.

It doesn't necessarily matter whether you start from head to foot or from foot to head. I like to re-awaken the muscles in the reverse order of how I relaxed them.

Step 3

Visualise a box, like a treasure chest, which has a lock on the front to which you hold the key. Imagine, with the box unlocked and lid opened, that stressful items are dropping into the box. You can place the printed name of the stressful activity or event on a slip of paper and watch it drop into the box. You can take an object or picture that represents the event also. See more and more of them falling into the box. At first, it is slow enough that you see the named events; later, it is such a downpour that you only see the names here and there. Your mind will then reduce the flow to a trickle, and then the last few.

Then gently close the lid, lock the box, and hold the key. Attach the box by the handle on the top to a 'clothesline' attached to a pulley. One end is near you, and the other is far off in the distance, too far to be seen. Hand over hand, reel the treasure chest or box away from you, on the clothesline, until it is out of sight. While doing this, realise that you could, if you wanted, reel it back in and use the key to unlock the box and revisit any stressful items stored inside at any time you want.

This concludes the visualisation. Some notes:

- You must be able to lock the box to secure the stressful thoughts and return them to your control. You do not throw away the key because you need to retain the right to control whether you want to visit these thoughts again. In fact, you may not ever want to but you need to have the choice.
- Also, some people are tempted to throw the box overboard into the ocean or tie it to a balloon that takes it out of sight. If you do this, be sure that the rope or anchor to which it is attached is within your grasp—you need to be able to recover it at any time, even though you do not do this during your visualisation.

Step 4

- 'Re-awakening the muscles' does not mean making them tense: it means restoring them to normal 'awakeness' and aliveness so that you are not groggy.

You will be amazed at how tolerant this makes you of stressful events at home or at work. That's right, at home too! Home life can create a lot of stresses— finances, raising children, and more; I suggest you retain the practice even if work is no longer your major source of stress.

Quick method

If you forget to do the thorough method, or are hit with a new project 'trauma', it is important to have a method that you can do quickly at work. After all, it is not necessarily easy for others to understand what you are doing if you start a 10–15 minute procedure in the office!

For example, you are on time and within budget in your new project. At a meeting, the executives tell you how important it is to have the project done by the end of the week! Of course, the original deadline was such that you thought you had at least two more months!

That is an example of something that might be a prescription for instant stress. You may need something to get you through the rest of the day. The following technique can be done with eyes open, even during a meeting, probably without anyone knowing it. It takes between a minute to a minute and a half.

It is called 'One–Ten–One'. It is based on the fact that when you are stressed, in addition to your muscles getting tense, your breathing often becomes shallow and rapid. Since the body also controls the mind, controlling the breath can control the mental tension.

Many of our body functions such as digestion and heartbeat are automatic (autonomic). It is true that being frightened may change our pulse and that thoughts therefore control it to a certain extent. However, most of us cannot simply decide to stop our heartbeat altogether.

Still other body functions are manual (voluntary), such as walking and moving your arms. You have complete control of your motion. One function in particular is both automatic and manual: the breath. You are entirely in conscious control of it but when asleep, you do not forget to breathe.

The breath responds automatically to stress, yet it can be controlled manually. This makes it an ideal tool to use for reducing stress quickly. The 1–10–1 technique makes use of timing of the breath.

How to do it:

1 Count first to one, and breathe in.
2 Then count one, two and take that long to breathe out.
3 Count one, two, three to breathe in.
4 Continue the out-breath to a four count, in to a five count.
5 Continue the in-out pattern up to the count of 10 (the longest breath).
6 Then breathe in to a nine count, out to the count of eight.
7 Reduce the counts and speed up the breath accordingly, back to one.

Keep the timing even and rhythmic, like a cadence. The higher the arithmetic progression of numbers, the longer it takes to breathe in and out. By making the breath more rapid than normal, then slower than normal, then faster again, you regain control of your breath timing that stress often puts out of control.

Common errors include trying to breathe in and out all at once, then waiting out the remaining timing of the cadence. Try to control the pace of the in and out breaths so that you are at the end of the in or out breath just as you get to the end of the count sequence.

Here is a pictorial view:

1 (in)

1 2 (out)

1 2 3 (in)

1 2 3 4 (out)

1 2 3 4 5 (in)

1 2 3 4 5 6 (out)

1 2 3 4 5 6 7 (in)

1 2 3 4 5 6 7 8 (out)

1 2 3 4 5 6 7 8 9 (in)

1 2 3 4 5 6 7 8 9 10 (out)

1 2 3 4 5 6 7 8 9 (in)

1 2 3 4 5 6 7 8 (out)

1 2 3 4 5 6 7 (in)

1 2 3 4 5 6 (out)

1 2 3 4 5 (in)

1 2 3 4 (out)

1 2 3 (in)

1 2 (out)

1 (in)

In summary, you can manage your stress through prevention techniques, such as a daily structured technique for doing the best job you can, and working on others' levels of initiative to bring things more under your control. If you forget, then correction techniques can be used. These include the thorough technique of progressive relaxation and visualisation, and the quick technique of 1–10–1.

Projects can seem very stressful to many people. This is a way of keeping that stress level under control.

And now, after you have practised the ideas in this chapter, and have done much to bring your own house in order, it is time to help others do the same.

3

Getting other's houses in order

Now that you have done a lot of work on yourself, it is time to look at interactions with people, including helping team members to be more effective.

We will look at:

- One on one dynamics
- Written communication
- Working with groups
- Handling negotiations, conflict, and criticism
- Effective staffing and work

9 One on one dynamics

- Good ideas + good implementation = success.
- The key to good implementation is good communications.
- The quality of your life is the quality of your communication.

GOOD COMMUNICATION

Many people have had experiences around a time when words seemed like magic. Maybe it was a public event like a speech by Martin Luther King or John F. Kennedy. Maybe it was a special teacher who praised you for an assignment or a parent or spouse who spoke with such precision and romance that the words stayed with you forever. I wonder which experience you would choose.

When John Grinder and Richard Bandler studied successful people, they found common attributes. One of the most important was precise communication skills. A manager has to manage information to be successful. Bandler and Grinder found that the most successful managers seemed to have a genius for getting to the heart of information rapidly and communicating to others what they had learned. They tended to use key phrases and words that conveyed important ideas with great precision.

Today, we are going to learn about tools that will help you communicate with more precision and effectiveness than you may ever have had before. You are going to learn how to guide others towards an important outcome.

We all learned speech at an early age. That is, we learned nouns and pronouns, grammar, etc. Few of us learned how to use words to communicate to others in a really meaningful way. It is amazing that years later (perhaps after numerous degrees) we have to find new ways to enhance that ability. Why is communication so important?

In today's world, power comes from specialised knowledge. In many countries, the kinds of specialised knowledge needed to transform the quality of our lives is available to everyone but knowledge alone is not enough. We must understand our own strengths and limitations (communicate with ourselves) and also be able to share our knowledge well with others. What we are talking about is first gaining power over ourselves, getting our own houses in order, before we use the power of knowledge in working with others.

The great leaders and communicators are simply very good at getting their message across. 'Exerting' power and coercion have only limited and temporary effectiveness and become unnecessary. You may change a person's mind or you may not; the point is, most success comes from being heard (understood) correctly in the first place. If it is a good idea that you have, it needs good implementation through good communication to lead to success, as the following pages show.

Good ideas

**plus
good
implementation**

equals success

Good communication is the

to good implementation

Now for the trip to the senior manager

The old way...

Orchestrating the new way...

Within your work area

why communicate like this?

when you can cooperate

ONE ON ONE DYNAMICS

The area of one on one dynamics is perhaps the single most important area in working with others. There are many times when we meet with others in a two-person meeting. Certainly, it is vitally important with families: between children, spouses, or both. Team members need to get together with each other and their project manager, with customers and with suppliers. The project manager needs to meet one on one with these people, plus other managers and executives within the organisation. This may include coaching people to be more motivated and proactive. If your personal meetings can be successful, most of the following sections will fall into place.

BUILDING RAPPORT

Rapport:

- is meeting others at their model of the world;
- is matching our communication output to the way the other person naturally inputs information;
- increases the likelihood that the message sent will equal the message received; and
- promotes trust and comfort among people who are communicating.

Rapport is fundamental to effective communication. We may feel that rapport is spontaneous and natural, and cannot be forced. There are ways, however, that we can learn to be in rapport, because we do not always do 'reliably' what often comes naturally.

Rapport can be accomplished verbally, by noting:

- the way a person uses speech (representation systems); and
- their voice, tone, tempo and pitch.

Rapport can also be achieved physically, by noting:

- body posture and gestures;
- breathing patterns;
- head position;
- facial movements;
- eye movements; and
- weight shifts and hand gestures.

It can also be done with content, by noting how a person sorts information (more about this later).

Finally, it can be done logically, by noticing if a person is talking about self-identity, beliefs, capabilities, behaviours, or environment.

This seems like a lot to learn!

All of these concepts are basically ways of practising *the main rule* which is:

• meet others at their model of the world.

This means finding out what the other's style is rather than worrying about your own. To meet others at their model of the world, you must put yourself in their shoes, and match them before leading them to where you would like them to be.

Think of it this way: in a discussion you already know what you are going to say, yet your listener is hearing it for the first time. It is better for you to slow down and translate it into your listener's language. Otherwise, he or she will 'space out' and miss key points (or even lose interest) if they have to struggle to translate from your system to theirs. You won't lose your place, because you know what you are going to say, so you can do all the work. They will lose their place if they are trying to comprehend and suddenly have to translate as well.

Let's look at these topics one by one. I will also include some powerful examples that make the point very effectively, and will also get you practised at the principles. If you practise, you will indeed improve your ability to build rapport. We will start right out with an exercise; see if you can grab at least two other people from your organisation or family to help you.

Exercise: Rapport

1 Count off by threes (if in a large group).
2 Person one remains in the room, as persons two and three leave temporarily. Person one, do not turn to the next page until after this exercise.
3 Person two will turn the page to get special instructions.
4 Then person three will turn to the page after that to get special instructions.
5 Then persons two and three will return to the room and person one will tell them a story.
6 When persons two and three come back, person one will tell a short (two minute) story of interest on any subject to the persons two and three of your triad. Person one, this is a one-way conversation, do not ask any questions.

Person Two only

(Persons one and three—for best effect, do not read this page)

You, person two, are to *act* as if you are paying attention to the story. In reality, though, you are paying no attention whatsoever. Perhaps you have actual practice at this, as when someone wants to tell you something and you don't want to appear rude, yet you don't want to hear it!

A good trick is to make eye contact and set up your body as if you are paying attention, and then daydream or play your favourite song in your mind, or perhaps think about work.

Person Three only

(Persons one and two—for best effect, do not read this page)

Your task is to *act* like you are not paying attention to what is being said. In fact, you are to actually pay close attention to every word.

Good techniques might be to break eye contact, doodle, seem to be preoccupied—whatever works for you.

Now read this page only when you are done with the exercise.

7 Person one, write down who you thought was paying the most attention.

8 Then, person one ask the person who you thought was paying the most attention to re-tell what you said.

9 Then, person one ask this of the person you thought was paying the least attention.

10 Then, ask persons two and three to divulge their secret assignments.

Now turn the page only when done with these steps.

If you are skipping this exercise for now, please skip the next page until you get to do it, so you will not spoil the effect.

Fascinating! Most people misjudge who was paying the most attention. What this shows is that the *appearance*, oddly enough, is usually stronger than the reality, proving that the symbolism of rapport is actually more powerful than the content. You might also find that persons two and three had some difficulty carrying out their assignments—that it was hard to comprehend for those who were supposed to, or that some of the story sunk in for those who were to ignore it. This proves that the mind and the body are connected in this way.

It also shows what a powerful negative signal is sent by the person who says, 'Oh, go on talking, don't worry—I can do this task while you are talking, I can do two things at once'. Even if they could (which is doubtful) it sends a message that you are not important enough to have them stop what they are doing to pay attention with their whole body. Remember this the next time you are tempted to 'do two things at once' in front of the speaker!

This exercise shows also the extent to which appearing to pay attention, and paying attention, are usually linked. In other words, rapport is natural. Only if things are not going well might you notice your behaviour. If it is important to get the content from someone you don't like, be sure you are physically in rapport first, and it will be easier. Conversely, you can stop taking in a 'toxic' conversation by breaking rapport with your body.

NLP PRESUPPOSITIONS

In Chapter 4, we discussed the value of NLP in helping you change habits. NLP is also the best way to gain an advanced knowledge of rapport building techniques. It has some very good assumptions, called presuppositions, that are seen as valuable truths about the world. If endorsed by project managers and team members, these presuppositions would result in outstanding communication:

1   The meaning of a communication is the response it elicits, regardless of the communicator's intention.

2   There are no failures in communication, only feedback and failures in responses.

3   The recognition of responses requires only that the five sensory channels are clean and open.

4   Individuals with the most flexibility are most likely to achieve the response they want.

5   People have all the resources necessary to make any desired change, and are always doing the best they can.

6   Individuals communicate both consciously and unconsciously.

7   All behaviour, even negative behaviour, has a positive intention behind it.

8   The map is not the territory.

9   Modelling successful performance leads to excellence.

10 Rapport is meeting people at their model of the world.

11 Resistance is a comment upon the inflexibility of the communicator.

Let us now have a look at how people process information. Remember, the more we match their systems, the more likely we are to build rapport and be understood. We will go into some detail; please don't worry if you feel you will not master it all! The more of this you can grasp and practise, the better you will be in rapport. Even picking up just some of the skills will help. Some of you will grasp certain areas more readily than others. Take the areas that are most comfortable for you.

REPRESENTATIONAL SYSTEMS

'To effectively communicate, we must realise that we are all different in the way we perceive the world and use this understanding as a guide to our communications with others.' ANTHONY ROBBINS

Representation systems are like the key to a secret code. Given normal neuro-physiological functioning, we experience the world, for the most part, through all our senses simultaneously. In order to deal with so much input, we naturally develop preferred sensory modalities to process information.

The main types are:

- visual;
- auditory;
- kinesthetic; and
- olfactory or gustatory.

The preferred system of an individual will be their most highly valued one. The preferred system will also be expressed in the person's use of language and in a part of grammar known as *predicates* (the active verb, together with the words it governs and those that might modify it, such as adverbs and adjectives).

You can identify the preferred representational system of individuals by listening to the predicates used in their speech. Once you can identify a system, you can use this information to enhance rapport by matching your predicates to the person's preferred system.

RECOGNISING PREFERRED SYSTEMS—VERBAL RAPPORT

Visual systems

Speech is usually fast and breathing high in chest. Tone is high pitched and may be strained. Muscle tension in shoulders and abdomen is prevalent. 'Visual' speakers have much tendency to point to things.

Examples

- This is how it looks to me.
- I can't picture myself doing that.
- I see what you mean.
- I am painting a clear picture.
- I take a dim view of your perspective.

Auditory systems

Speech is more modulated, tempo is balanced and the voice has clarity with resonant tonality. Breathing is even and deep, coming from the diaphragm or whole chest. If the person folds hands or arms, it usually indicates auditory accessing.

Examples

- I hear what you are saying.
- It sounds suspicious to me.
- That rings a bell.
- That does not resonate with me at all.
- I want to say this loud and clear.

Kinesthetic systems

Speech is at a slow tempo, with low, deep tonality and long pauses between words. Posture tends to be solid.

Examples

- Are you able to get a handle on this?
- I feel like I'm in touch with what you are saying.
- It doesn't feel right to me.
- I want to get a grasp on this.
- I'm not sure I'm following you.

Other systems

Less frequently found are olfactory and gustatory:

Examples

- Something smells fishy here.
- This leaves a bad taste in my mouth.

Also, systems may be unspecified (sometimes called *generic* or *digital*). Digital representational systems may be common among technical or scientific people.

Examples

- I understand what you say.
- I want to communicate something.
- I am aware of your dilemma.
- I notice the quality of your report.
- I comprehend the difficulties.

When you know someone's main representational system, you have taken a large step toward entering it. All you have to do is match it.

For example, consider someone who is primarily in an auditory state. If you are trying to persuade him to do something by asking him to picture how it will look, and you talk very rapidly in a high tone of voice, you probably won't get through to him. He needs to hear what you have to say, listen to your proposal and notice if it clicks for him.

To make a powerful point: many apparent 'personality conflicts' result from people using different representational systems—they are not really conflicts at all.

An associate and I were driving to the airport in San Francisco. I was predominantly visual and kinesthetic, and she was primarily auditory. Our conversation went something like, 'Look at the overhead sign and you will see the directions' from me followed by, 'You are not hearing what I am saying' from my associate. She dropped me off at the kerb, where I was going to check in and then return to the car, but there was no place to park. I suggested she just follow the signs to return to the airport. When I came back, she did not return for considerable time. It turned out that she headed in the wrong direction, blocked the traffic, and needed auditory directions from a police officer to get back to the airport!

In the next few days listen to people you are talking to and determine what words they use most. Speak to them in the same representational system. Selecting words (predicates) to match others' representational systems is called using predicate systems.

As an aid, you will notice that a person's eye movements are usually related to the thinking process they are using (visual, auditory or kinesthetic) (see diagram). Further, you can even tell whether they are constructing something, remembering something or talking to themselves (known as auditory dialogue). The following diagram shows how a right-handed person's eyes would appear to you as they process information in different ways. For left handed people, the left/right patterns are reversed (about 90% of the time). Some people have large eye movements, and others less.

Eye Accessing Clues

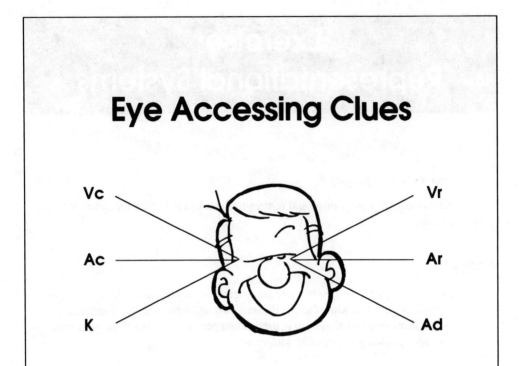

Key

Vc: visual, constructing

Vr: visual, remembering

Ac: auditory, constructing

Ar: auditory, remembering

K: kinesthetic

Ad: auditory, dialogue

Exercise: Representational Systems

(For a group of people)

Divide into groups of three and remain in these triads for the following exercise phases.

Phase 1

Person one makes up two or three sentences in one particular set of predicates (visual, auditory, or kinesthetic). Persons two and three attempt to determine which representational system is used. Then persons two and three have turns so that each person gets to create sentences.

Phase 2

Person one makes up three sentences using all three major representational systems in a certain random, unstated sequence. Persons two and three answer person one using three different sentences, yet using the same three representational systems in the same order as stated by person one. Then all people rotate as in Phase 1.

Notice that you may feel more comfortable with one of the three different styles. Note which person and which style, for later analysis.

Phase 3

Person one makes up one or two paragraphs having perhaps eight to ten sentences in all, speaking without regard to particular representational systems (ie speaking as one would normally). Persons two and three attempt to determine the representational system favoured instinctively by person one. Then all people rotate as in Phase 1.

Exercise: Translation

Remain in triads as for the previous exercise. Then, note each person's most favoured representational system. Use also the comfort level obtained in Phase 2 of the previous exercise to help you with this identification.

For each pair of people with differing representational systems, the third person acts as a 'translator', as in the following example:

Person one, who is auditory, says four or five sentences in her favoured (auditory) predicate systems to person two.

Person two, noting that person three is visual, translates the content into visual predicates and re-explains the same paragraph to person three in visual rather than auditory terms.

Each person switches so that all get turns at all roles. If two or more preferred representational systems are the same, change one so that everyone gets a turn at translating into a different system.

MATCHING AND LEADING

As we have already covered to some extent, matching a person's favoured system can be very important. This is the point of building rapport, both verbal and physical using strategies, metaphors and so forth.

What if the person with whom you are working has an uncomfortable posture for you, or speaks at an uncomfortable rate? Can you simply start out at your favoured pace and assume you will be matched? This is very unlikely, since he or she has probably not studied this material; you are the only one that you can ultimately change.

There is a temptation to discount another person, to believe that they ought not act the way they do, and communicate accordingly. If you do this, however, you will fail to communicate. As Anthony Robbins puts it, '…it is tempting to assume that the person is a hopeless fool that refuses to listen to reason' when you fail to communicate with someone. This attitude will virtually guarantee that you'll never get through. It is simply better to change what you do until it matches the other's representational systems and model of the world. You always have that choice.

When matching and leading, you must match before you can lead even if you are uncomfortable doing so.

There is a more important reason to lead than your comfort or physical position. If you have a contrary view on a subject, find an area of agreement first if possible, then lead into another area. You will be unable to lead if you do not match first.

How about dealing with anger and rage, hyperactivity or other uncomfortable situations? In many cases, it is helpful at least to match the pace and intensity of the dialogue, and then move to a calmer place. Be certain that you do not get caught up in the furore yourself. In other cases, rapid deflection and diffusing the situation may be best, an example of *pattern breaking*. Another manoeuvre is *reframing*. For example, a reporter, attempting to confront Ronald Reagan with his advancing age when he was running for the presidency, asked: 'Excuse me, but don't you think age will be a factor in this election?' The response was a deflection: 'I don't think my opponent's youth will harm him'.

Exercise: Pacing

(For groups)

Divide into pairs. Person one turns to the next page for special instructions (Person two, do not turn the page).

Then, upon return, person one engages person two in a conversation as per instructions.

When done with the two- or three-minute conversation, person one please invite person two to read the instructions, and discuss what you did and its effects.

Person one instructions

(Person two—do not read until after the exercise)

You are to engage in an interactive conversation with person two. During the two-way conversation, gradually accelerate your pace and notice if they follow. Then gradually reduce the pace and notice if they follow as well. After the conversation, discuss what happened.

Exercise: Matching

Divide into pairs for this exercise.

With one of you speaking and the other listening, try to avoid this 'out of rapport' situation.

And choose this one instead.
After matching, switch places.

Exercise: Being heard

Divide into pairs. Study the following paragraph, which is typical of something commonly accepted by Quality Assurance (QA) people, and often not really seen or accepted by peers, developers or senior management.

'Quality Assurance is a necessary part of our organisation. By making sure the job is done right the first time, even with added cost at the front end, the entire job is completed with higher quality and lower cost in the long run. Just notice how the cost of prevention and appraisal is so much smaller than the cost of failure. We can effect these improvements by designing improved quality control systems, measuring and monitoring, and testing throughout the development life cycle rather than at the very end'.

A typical reaction to this paragraph, by people seeing QA as a meddling, delaying, costly, overhead process might be this.

Your job is to instil this in your listener.

First, have your listener speak to you long enough to calibrate to their representational systems. Then, using the techniques you have learned, reframe the paragraph in such a way that it can be heard, then tell your listener. Finally, switch partners so each gets a turn.

SORTING STYLES

Up to this point, we have discussed the somewhat 'microscopic', or detailed, aspects of rapport. By now, you notice it is far more than just what used to be called 'body language'. We use 'micro' because we look not at the meaning behind the sentences; rather, we understand (with predicates, for example) what they mean when they stand alone.

When we look at how people process information on a greater scale, we see ways in which they sort predicate usage (strategies) and tendencies of affinity in language (sorting styles). These are more like the sentence by sentence meanings rather than the word by word and, instead of microscopic, are 'medium'-scopic (I just coined a word!)

Some different ways in which people 'sort', or have an affinity or preference, for information are listed below. When matching, you will want to notice which of the many sorting styles listed below are used by your listener, and then frame the meanings of your sentences in that way as much as you can.

The listed words indicate the principal meaning or usage of the sentences used a listener to sort information. For example, if the sorting style is 'people', then that person will tend to describe most situations in terms of how different people participate. Similarly, a 'places' person will categorise chiefly by where events take place. One who sorts by 'time' will tend to outline the events that take place in the sequence in which they occurred.

- People, places things (Generally, people sort principally for one of these three things, or none of them)
- Activities or information
- Curiosity (or not)
- Match/mismatch
- General/specific
- Self/other
- Positive/negative
- Internal/external
- Approach/avoidance
- Time (or not)
- Modality (strength of preference for visual, auditory or kinesthetic processing)
- Meta-model distinctions (fine shades of meaning and exact definitions)
- Procedures or options (The willingness to follow procedures versus the need to be creative and unstructured. By the way, procedures-sort folk are best at

following but not writing procedures. Options-sort folk are best at creating procedures but not following them!)

- Concept (theory) followed by structure (procedure) followed by use (example). (Nearly everyone does all three of these, however the order of performance varies from individual to individual. A C-S-U (concept-structure-use) sort person needs the theory first, then can work out the procedure and form the example later, if they need to. A U-S-C sort person needs to see the example before they can figure the process, then they finally see the theory behind it. All sort orders of CSU are possible. Most high executives are both visual and C-S-U. Many technical contributors are auditory and U-S-C or S-U-C).

Now, how do you match a mismatcher? No, it is not an oxymoron but refers to contrary or rebellious types. You can use words such as, 'You wouldn't want to do it this way, would you?' or tell them what they want to avoid. This moves them in the direction you want them to go.

I was once told how one of the participants in my class would be incorrigible— that there was no way he would learn anything about quality. He was against everything. I took this on as a challenge. I spent the seminar telling him that he had to be against anything that was non-quality. He became the most ferocious 'bulldog' for quality in the whole organisation. He systematically did a 'seek and destroy' mission to ferret out anything that stood in his way that was not quality, and he became the leading quality champion in the organisation!

LOGICAL LEVELS

If physical patterns and predicates are at the 'micro' level, and sorts are at the 'medium' level, then logical levels are at the 'macro' level. If the word is micro, and the sentence is medium, then the concept behind a series of sentences is the logical level.

After listening to a paragraph or so, you can principally tell whether a person is relating to their sense of:

- identity, or 'who', (highest level);
- what they believe in, which is 'why';
- what they are capable of, which is 'what';
- the behaviour needed to do something, which is 'how'; or
- the environment in which the behaviour is done—'where' or 'when'.

You want to match a person on this greatest, or macroscopic level, as well. Conflict is usually the result of two people saying the same things, and being at different logical levels. The solution is to match: each person can try to 'jump up' to the highest level of either, continue to move slowly up until there is agreement, then both move slowly down. We will say more on this subject with an example in the section on criticism and conflict later in this chapter. Here is a pictorial view of the levels.

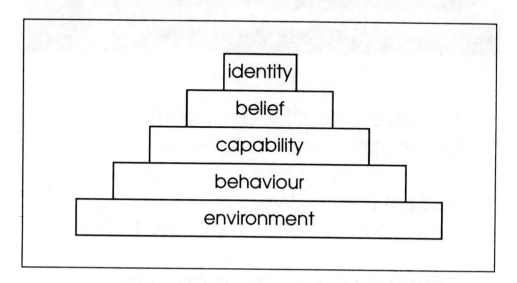

PATTERN CATEGORIES

The levels of rapport are summarised below, although some we will not discuss much in this book. They range from the micro to the macro:

- Physical patterns
- Modalities and submodalities. V, A, and K are modalities; submodalities are gradients of each. For example, gradients of V, A, and K are: fuzzy/clear, loud/soft, and sharp/dull respectively.
- Strategies (recall, sequence of modalities)
- Sorting styles
- Metaphors (stories or analogies to make a point)
- Beliefs
- Logical levels

BEING AN EFFECTIVE LISTENER

Armed with these new rapport tools, here are some steps to better listening. Now that you have helped the other person to listen to you more, it is only fair that you be able to do the same.

Six steps to managing an effective communication

Perceive difficulties as opportunities
for creating something new

Accent the positive:
state your outcome in positive terms

Create an evidence procedure:
how will I know it when I see it?

Institute a measurable outcome

Note use of assumptions:
when doubt and distrust are present,
check assumptions

Get curious, not furious:
ask questions to gain new information

P   A   C   I   N   G   yourself

Seven steps of listening

Concentrating

Acknowledging

Responding

Exercising emotional control

Sensing

Structuring

Sequencing
    Active listening:
    • paraphrase
    • clarify
    • feedback
    Listen with empathy,
    openness and awareness.

Blocks to Listening

Comparing

Mind-reading

Rehearsing

Filtering

Judging

Dreaming

Identifying

Advising

Sparring

Being right

Derailing

Placating

A WORD ON ACTIVE LISTENING

In this brief review of active listening techniques for project people, here are the key things to remember:

1 Listening can be very intense and even tiring if you are really, really listening. Most people hear perhaps 20% of what is said. With a lot of work, you may get it up to 50%.

2 Anything that sets your mind off on a tangent, thinking about something else, interferes with listening. The 'Blocks to Listening' above are nothing other than 12 ways of keeping the mind busy with something other than paying attention.

3 To actively listen, you must be ready to ask questions when you don't understand (quite natural for many of us, especially in technical fields). You must, however, also be prepared to frequently paraphrase back to the speaker, even when you do understand what was said. This is a growth area for many people. Only then can the speaker 'quality control' check your understanding.

4 The speaker has an obligation too. You can organise and structure what you are saying in an orderly way, general to specific, so that it can be heard. I suggest you look for visual cues to see if your listener is 'lost in space'. Put in frequent pauses in case you don't notice these cues, so that the listener can interject a question without feeling they are interrupting rudely.

WALKING IN THE OTHER'S SHOES

Once you have worked on your rapport and listening skills, it is time to realise that 'meeting others at their model of the world' really means 'walking in their shoes'. All of the NLP techniques above are helpful for doing that in a technical way. You also need to do this in an emotional way, far broader and deeper than individual language techniques alone. You really want to understand what it is like being in their position, going through what they go through in a day.

Many of us master walking in our own shoes, and are not very good at walking in other's. From the powerful NLP presupposition, 'the meaning of a communication is the response it elicits' we can take a new view. This presupposition means that it doesn't matter how well we did (in theory); all that matters is: did the other person's behaviour change? When you think of it, most communication is with the hoped-for outcome that the other's behaviour or attitude will change in some way as a result.

Despite this, ask yourself this question very honestly: when we walk in to talk to someone, are we principally thinking of what we want to say or have happen? Or are we principally thinking of how our words are going to be heard? Maybe for most of us it is what we are going to say. And yet it is clear that the meaning of a communication is what is experienced by the other person, not by you. In other words, most of us get this exactly backwards!

This is especially important in families. Parents often forget what it was like growing up, and fail to see things from their child's perspective. All the exercises in this section apply equally well to family members.

Try out this exercise:

Awareness Exercise

Scene 1

In your mind, try to remember the last time you had an agenda and you walked into someone's office space. You had on your mind what you wanted to do with project XYZ (meanwhile, they were saturated with their own project ABC). You needed help, and had this in mind as you saw them. What were your thoughts?

Scene 2

Now let that scene clear, and pick another scene. In this one, you were seated in your office space, up to your neck in project ABC. You were already behind schedule and over budget perhaps, or attending to a project emergency of some sort. In walks another person who wants help with their project XYZ. Did you focus on them? Were you just trying to be polite, secretly glancing at your watch, hoping they would leave? Did you nod, signifying acceptance, and really not want to be bothered?

If you had a different experience the second time from the first, it is because you remembered what it was like being in the position of being asked.

Scene 3

Now clear the scene again, and remember a time similar to the second scene. You are seated in your office space, again overburdened with project ABC, and in walks a person wanting assistance with XYZ. This time, despite your pressures, you find yourself drawn in to the conversation and willing to help. What was the difference? Did they match you, acknowledging how you were overloaded, first? Did they instead show you how your help in project XYZ would also have results that would help you with your project ABC? What was the difference?

Your goal, of course, is to walk in the other's shoes such that your experience is not different from scene one to scene two.

Here is an interesting exercise that can drive home the principle of walking in the other's shoes—literally!

Physical Rapport Exercise

Pair off by twos, and for the next 15 minutes person one will lead and person two will follow and model—exactly!!!

Then switch, so person two will lead and person one will follow and model, for the next 15 minutes.

Remember that if you start out this way, for the first 15 minutes...

...then this may be the way it will go for the last 15!!!

You may have noted from the modeling exercise how the mind and body often track one another. The very first exercise in this chapter, on rapport, introduced you to the importance of these often subconscious cues. What was once called 'body language' (a subset of physical rapport) has tremendous communicative ability. It can help to make a person feel either very comfortable or uncomfortable, and therefore increase or decrease the ease and flow of communication.

Some further points:

- Mirroring is a natural process of rapport.
- Note the difference between mimicking and modelling.
- We do much of this instinctively and naturally, although not always reliably; understanding physical rapport can help start these difficult situations flowing once again.
- Rapport creates a commonality of physiology that underscores our shared reality.
- Benefits include direct experience of another person's feelings, experiences and thoughts without being invasive.
- We tend to trust people who appeal to us on all levels and give off a sense of congruity (where all parts of a personality convey the same thing).

You may have had a new, heightened awareness of 'literally' being in the other person's shoes. Little things you may not have noticed before become extremely apparent. Perhaps it was difficult or distracting to pay enough attention in order to model the other person exactly. Perhaps you were even judging their behaviour. This is a great 'training' exercise to heighten your awareness of others.

A word about judgements: many people have a fear that there is a danger in trying to understand emotionally where another is coming from. The danger is that if they understand, they have to agree with them or their behaviour. They think, 'Maybe I don't want to agree! Maybe if I understand, I will be forced to!'.

Wrong!

You can understand deeply why somebody commits a crime, such as killing someone, without accepting that it is right, or deciding to be a killer yourself. Deep empathy for the other's position cannot hurt you—it can only help you.

So, on this 'gas gauge' of understanding, you do not actually run the risk of 'crossing over' the double line.

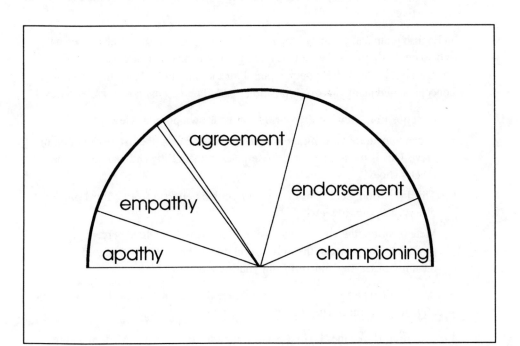

PERCEPTUAL POSITIONS

Let's have a more in-depth view of walking in the other's shoes, from a variety of perspectives.

In English grammar, you may have heard the terms 'first person', 'second person' and so on. Perhaps you heard it in relation to sentence structure, such as 'first person singular' and 'third person plural' or the like. In NLP, we have a similar concept, stated using the word 'position', called perceptual positions, as follows:

- First position: viewing the world from your own point of view.
- Second position: viewing the world from the other's (the listener's) point of view. This is the position in the exercises in modelling and walking in the other's shoes.
- Third position: seeing both you and your listener(s) from a third party observer's point of view.
- Meta position: there is a meta position for each of the three perceptual positions. For projects, the most useful one is the meta position to first, meaning observing yourself from your own point of view.

These are called perceptual positions because they are mental positions that you perceive in your mind. They are ways of seeing.

First position is like the 'I' (first person singular) in grammar. Most of us are masters at this position, so this is not a problem. We usually see things from our own point of view, to begin with. For projects, this is the least useful position to spend most of your thinking time in. In the swish technique, this is the associated, old picture, looking through your own eyes.

Second position is like the 'you' (second person singular or plural) in grammar. This is walking in the other's shoes, and is essential for any teaching activity or one-on-one communication or convincing activity with anyone. Since, from the NLP presuppositions, the meaning of a communication is the response it elicits, this is called speaking the other's language. In a sense, all activities related to predicates, eye patterns, sorting styles, and logical levels are simply detailed ways of analysing the second position of another.

Third position is like the 'they' (third person plural) in grammar. This is how a camera would view the two of you, or all of you, in a meeting or group. It is sometimes nicknamed the 'observer' position. In the swish technique, you are in third position (dissociated) in the new picture because you see all of you as well as the other participants. This is most useful for facilitation and conflict resolution, because you observe the entire dynamic. Have you ever seen two or more people involved in an argument, or go off the track in a meeting discussion, which was so clear to you yet not to them? If so, you were physically in the observer position, and they were so wrapped up in first or second position that they could not see themselves.

Meta position is really a third position, or observer position, to any of the three perceptual positions above. It is excellent for self-evaluation and improvement. For example, after facilitating a meeting, you can take meta position to first, in order to observe how you behaved and to 'comment' on it in your mind.

Each of us have been in these positions, physically. We know what standing in our shoes, with our worries and concerns, is like. We have also been participants in seminars or listeners on 'the other side of the fence'. Especially if we had a speaker or seminar leader just like us to observe this way, we have had a first-hand 'dose' of what it is like to be on the receiving end. Perhaps we glimpsed how we would have sounded to others. And we have perhaps walked in late to a meeting, or observed as a non-participant, and seen a dynamic that the meeting members have not.

When we discussed visualisation in Chapter 4, we noted that there is very little difference between what is visualised with great accuracy and what is actually done. In the same way, we can imagine with great accuracy that we are listening to ourselves in second or third or meta position, as if we were physically standing in that position. Excellent instructors are thinking of what they are going to say (first position) and, as they are saying it, listening for the way in which it is heard at the same time (second position). During class participation, they are also observing the entire class interaction as an observer would see it (third position), like a 'fly on the wall'. Excellent facilitators are concerned with the content too, of course. They are watching, as an observer, the entire overall dynamic to make sure dysfunctional behaviours are handled effectively and that the content stays on track with the agenda.

Now to have a look at a special way of improving your skills at second and third position:

Exercise: Perceptual position

This takes two people. If you have a third, they can participate and observe in rotation.

1 Form pairs, with paired chairs facing one another. We will call you persons A and B. An optional third party observer can sit between, off to the side, so that they can observe both of you.

2 A converses with B and B converses with A; A gets up and sits in B's chair and relates to the empty A chair as if he/she were B (second position). While A is doing this, B is standing and watching from the side. When done, both explore what happened. Any observer can also comment about the entire dynamic.

3 Both are seated, both converse, and this time B gets up (ie the roles are reversed).

4 Both are seated, both converse, and both get up and comment from third position.

5 If you are using three people, you can rotate so that the observer gets a turn as well.

It's amazing what goes on here. Many of you will get a sudden, full bodied experience as you sit down in the other's chair and try to become them (gestures, talking style, everything). Many of you will literally 'know' what it is like for the other person. The exercise forces this awareness.

Now of course in 'real' life you do not get to literally switch positions physically like this. Nor, when you are presenting, can you interrupt yourself, saying, 'Just a moment', and then take a seat in the audience! So why do this technique?

By experiencing what it is like, and continuing to imagine, and practising this exercise, you will become better and better at second and third position, because your mind will know how to do it and what it feels like.

Now, you are ready for another NLP process that I developed that you can do yourself, called 'A day in the life of the other person'. It is a comprehensive exercise in second position that can be done at work or home. It is valuable in situations like these:

- You gave someone a direction or instruction, and they either didn't do it, or reacted dramatically or very negatively to you as a result (much to your surprise).
- You are about to meet with your new project team, and see the team members in this context for the first time and want to make a great first impression.
- You are meeting with a manager, supplier, or customer for the first time.
- You have just a brief time to make your point, and don't have a second chance; you want to increase the likelihood that you will be understood and supported.
- You are about to conduct a presentation and have just one chance to be profoundly effective in a short time.
- You have a need to discipline (or have a frank discussion) with your children and want it to be heard in a way that is effective, non-threatening, and non-judgemental.

Because you actually have experienced what the other person has gone through, the technique below is especially powerful. This experience could have happened in a number of ways. You could have actually been in their position in the past. Or, you've observed their behaviour over a period of time. Even for a person you have never met, you may have met folk like them in a similar job position or can imagine what it would be like. All of this is locked up in our mind somewhere; it is just easy to forget. This technique 'unearths' these old, stuck memories, even if subconscious, as resources. The technique works so well, some will think you have a crystal ball! Of course, no mind-reading is required: all you are doing is capturing what the vast resource of your mind has to offer through its memories.

Exercise: A day in the life of the other person

This visualisation takes three to five minutes and you can do it in a place and at a time when you will be undisturbed. Some of you may visualise better with eyes closed. Unlike the swish pattern, what you see will be vignettes or movies, not still pictures. Do this as close to the time of the upcoming meeting as possible.

0   Re-live the past: (Optional step—to be used when correcting a past communication misunderstanding.) Remember, in detail, the misunderstanding. Paint a clear picture of the room or area, surroundings, other people. Hear the sounds, and feel what you felt. Remember how they were, what you said or did, their reaction, and your response to their reaction, in actions and feelings as well.

1   Go back a day: Go back about one day before the present time. For past misunderstandings, this is one day before that event; for new situations, one day before the upcoming meeting in the future.

Imagine, as accurately as you can, what it would be like to actually be the other person. (Deeply second position—remember, this can't hurt you). See yourself, as them, going through their day, with their project pressures, working at their station, interacting with their friends and associates. Get a sense of what it is like for them (as you, now). Picture going home, meeting with their family, overnight, next morning, breakfast, and on into work. Continue the detailed picture right up to the time of the past or future interaction.

If you have not yet seen this person, or know very little about them, make up the scene based on your knowledge. For example, if it is a supplier, imagine when you were a supplier, or experiences from other suppliers of the same nature. If it is a presentation, group the people into two or three different types, and imagine and remember the needs of people of that nature from your past experience.

What you don't know, make up: you are writing a screenplay. In family situations, for example with children, actually be that child for the day.

2 See the event as them: Now, the moment has come. Remember, you are still them. In comes a person with your name and face (you), saying or doing what you said (past, for misunderstandings) or are going to say (future, for new situations). As them, note now your reaction. You can have some new insights, provided you really do this process with integrity.

3 See it again as you: Switch back into your own skin (first position). Briefly replay the past or future scene from your point of view. Now note the composite of your reactions or expectations, coupled with the memory of their reactions.

4 Check, re-tool outcomes: If the outcome is as you hoped for, you are done. This may be true for the future situation, or it may not be. Of course it is not yet true when looking at past misunderstandings; further trials may be needed.

If you are not done, construct a new trial from step 3, in first position, saying or doing something different. Use your new knowledge of what it is like for them in order to reduce the number of trials needed. Replay the scene. Keep trying new interactions, in your mind, until you get the outcome you want.

Each of the techniques mentioned so far in this section on one-on-one dynamics may seem new and unique. Indeed, they may even seem strange. Perhaps at a party, if you were to mention them, people may actually start to back away from you in disbelief! I acknowledge how much change this represents, and I include them for only one reason—they work! So, don't *knock knock* it until you have *tried tried* it!

MANAGING YOUR BOSS

A rather presumptuous title, to be sure, and a necessary one: Good, effective managers want you to know how to make them look good. For team members, this includes your ability to work effectively with your project manager. No matter where you are in the hierarchy, almost everyone reports to someone. Even the CEO, Managing Director or General Manager has someone, perhaps the board of directors, and eventually their customers.

In the event that you had a little difficulty with the NLP techniques above, or they represented a little too much change for you, the traditional techniques in this topic may appeal to you.

The ability to influence those in higher positions is one of the most important yet difficult areas of communication for the effective manager. You may believe in and practise good two-way communication with your peers or with those who work for them, but how can you reach those for whom you work?

Three factors in particular to consider in sending messages they will listen to and act upon are their:

- significant others,
- filter categories, and
- managerial communication styles.

Significant others

To be more influential, become one of the 'significant others' for the person you wish to influence.

In an average day your manager will have substantial communication with between 15 and 25 people. Some of these will be *significant others*, ie people to whom your boss listens carefully and is likely to be influenced by. (This does not mean significant other in the romantic or marital sense!) Your goal is to become such a significant other (if you are not one already) that you can positively influence outcomes, including correct decisions on your project's budget and schedule, for example.

A In an average day a manager listens to an average of three such significant others.

B In general, the manager's boss will be one of the significant others for him or her, yet they themselves often will not be a significant other for the boss. To be influential, you must become a significant other for those above you.

C Identify the significant others for the people you wish to influence and study them. Are there ways in which you can exhibit the attitudes and actions that characterise such persons?

D Make yourself useful—'indispensable' if possible. Be more prepared than you are expected or required to be. Seek responsibility and do so in a manner that is supportive rather than competitive with your boss. See that your efforts reflect well on your boss and your group, as well as on yourself. Giving credit to others is often the most effective way of increasing the amount you receive yourself.

E I like to use a matrix for each of the managers that I want to influence. On one axis are the names of those I notice are significant others at my level, and on the other axis are behaviours exhibited by those people. There are patterns common to all; these are the patterns I want to emulate with integrity to become a significant other.

Manager Name / Significant Other	Socialises-builds rapport	Sends memo first	Keeps to the point	Walks in their shoes	
Name 1	✗		✗	✗	
Name 2	✗	✗	✗		
Name 3	✗	✗	✗	✗	
Name 4	✗				

By looking at this matrix, I determine that starting an interaction socially, building rapport, and perhaps keeping to the point will be the most valuable traits.

Filter categories

These are groupings of information which, through our experience, we come to deem important and give most attention to. Appeals to your manager's categories tend to be most effective in influencing them. The way we store processed information, ie memory, is an important consideration in this.

A Short-term memory: 8–12 hours. Information here is stored sequentially. If information you provide is stored here by your boss and you do not somehow relate it to his filter categories in some manner, it will be lost no matter how interesting or important it may be to you.

B Long-term memory: Retained after 12 hours. This information is stored topically. You are most likely to influence your boss if you provide *new* information that enhances his or her filter categories in long-term memory.

One who is not a significant other of the person they wish to influence can increase their ability to influence them by:

- identifying the *filter categories* of those they wish to reach and designing their messages accordingly;
- providing *new information*; your boss is more likely to be influenced by something not heard before than by repetition of things already known from other sources; and
- providing suggestions for *new courses of action*.

Managerial communication styles

There are a number of different styles by which managers receive and give information. Taking your boss's predominant style into consideration when designing messages meant to persuade him or her will make that message much more effective.

The Owl
Analytical style (decisive, delegator, gives feedback).

- Strengths: owls tend to be logical, systematic, thorough, critical, serious, precise.
- How to influence: give them new information; become an important information resource for them; owls crave as much data as possible before making decisions.

Operationalise for them. Be an actor, a 'can do' person for them. Often analysers are not good at getting things done and would rely on and appreciate those who can.

The Eagle
Driver style (planner, operationaliser, an actor; a person who prefers to do things rather than talk about them).

- Strengths: eagles tend to be independent, pragmatic, candid, determined, decisive, efficient.
- How to influence: show objective results they can see (give data, not just opinion).

Show them the consequences of different courses of action (alternatives and possible results of each).

The Dove
Amicable managerial style (strong interest in group cohesion).

- Strengths: doves tend to be cooperative, diplomatic, loyal, supportive, patient, respectful.
- How to influence: doves strongly value the opinions of others. In fact, they may tend to be overly influenced by the opinions of others. Show that your idea is well thought of by others—this is especially effective if the 'others' are seen as opinion leaders or significant others of the person.

This type of leader takes pride in others and their achievements, ie they generally like to see their subordinates or workgroup receive recognition and reward. Therefore, show how your ideas will reflect well on the program in general and others involved. Also indicate how the action you desire will increase cooperative effort and group morale.

The Peacock
Expressive managerial style (informal, anti-bureaucratic, with a good deal of interest shown in new things and approaches).

- Strengths: peacocks are imaginative, outgoing, friendly, enthusiastic, spontaneous.
- How to influence: Show uniqueness and innovation of the ideas you present.

Be enthusiastic yourself about the idea, not just analyse or show how good it is. Peacocks also particularly like to do things that will reflect well on themselves. Point out how their support of your idea will gain them recognition.

Other styles
While the above are examples of managerial styles, some schools of thought class people (whether managers or not) as oriented toward *power*, *affiliation* or *achievement*. It may be helpful for you to recognise these general categories as well.

10 Written communication

Communication and interaction are not just personal. Projects have a substantial need for written communication. Operating instructions and user manuals are examples. Interim and final project status reports, memos, shared data, and many other forms of writing can be found in projects. The recent explosion of faxes and e-mail, often used instead of long distance travel, places even more pressure to get this form of communication right.

While this is not a writing course, there are several key avenues I have seen that lead to difficult and clumsy writing styles, especially among project team members in technical areas.

First, use the rule 'Perfection is not desired'. This is easily mis-understood. If, sentence by sentence, you try to be 100% accurate in your writing and cover every contingency, you will miss the mark. Your sentences will be so long and written in such 'legalese' that no one will be able to understand them. Remember that human beings are not computers: a computer might understand your language if it is programmed to cover all bases, but could a human? Practise saying 80% of the key point in each sentence. Start with something that is mostly right, leaving out the exceptions. Then state the exceptions. Then use a metaphor or analogy, and add illustrations or examples. In fewer words, there will be much more clarity.

Second, to improve clarity, watch out for two enemies found commonly in writing style: passive verbs and noun phrases. Replace passive verbs with active verbs in the present tense. Sentences are easier to read if action-oriented, beginning with the action word (verb), and placed in the here and now (today). Using nouns instead of verbs, to form noun phrases, increases complexity too. Compare 'the communication of...' with 'communicate with...' or even 'speak to...'. Similarly, 'the establishment of ...' is harder than 'establish a...' or even 'create...'.

Third, you might want to use your favourite word-processor add-on to check what is called the 'Fog Index' of your work. The Fog Index is a number proportional to the difficulty of understanding of the work. It is equal to the grade level in school that a reader must be complete to have a chance of understanding it. The longer the sentence, and the more multi-syllable words per sentence, the higher (and worse) the index.

Even if a reader has attended a lot of school there is no reason to jack up the complexity. Although they are capable of understanding complex writing, it may not be easy for them.

Fog Index formula

The Fog Index is calculated as follows:

1 Count the average number of words per sentence in a paragraph of 100 words or more (= total word count / number of sentences).

2 Count the number of hard words (those having three syllables or more) and express as a percentage of the total.

3 Add 1 and 2 above and multiply by 0.4 to get the Fog Index. The smaller the index value, the better.

4 Use this rule for counting: a sentence ends with a period (.), a semicolon (;) or a comma (,) immediately followed by and, but, for, or.

5 Hard word rules: do not count as three syllables words ending in the suffixes -ed or -es; count acronyms as if spelled out.

6 Formula summary:

Fog Index = (average words per sentence + % hard words) * 0.4

Example:

100 word paragraph, 9 sentences, 12 hard words:

average words per sentence = 100/9 = 11.

% hard words = 12/100 = 12 %

Fog = (11 + 12) * 0.4 = 9.2

Exercise: Fog Index

Quickly read the following paragraph once (the way you would a novel), then close the book and tell someone else what it said.

> The Systems Manager receives the request for MIS services, prepares a preliminary estimate and returns the request to the MIS User. If the MIS Request does not contain enough information or the project is over 20 employee days, the Systems Manager can return the request for services to the MIS User requesting an External Design Report. However, if the project is over 20 employee days because several small projects are being 'bundled' in order to make the request more expedient, the 20 employee day guideline would be waived.

Pretty difficult, isn't it? The Fog Index of this paragraph is a little over 16. I have seen some writing with an index of 26! Of course, I don't know anyone who has graduated from the 26th grade!

I know people who try to write this way to convince others of their prowess. However, writing in a complex way does not make you seem more intelligent. It is not evidence of your wisdom. Quite the contrary: great masters of our day (Albert Einstein, Max Planck) were able to put very complicated theories into very simple language. Even the mission of the USA's National Aeronautics and Space Administration (NASA) in the 1960s was: to put a man on the moon. This is very simple language, indeed, for one of the most complex projects ever undertaken. In fact, each word in the mission is no more than one syllable!

11 Working with groups

Groups of people (your entire project team, a class, a presentation group, meetings) are really a general case of the one on one situations. In other words, when you understand how to accomplish one on one techniques described above, you are armed with what you need to know for groups, except for the additions contained in this section.

Each of the principles mentioned so far for individuals also applies to groups. When we combine the principles of NLP with ownership and good salesmanship, and apply it to groups of people, we also have effective teaching.

When teaching or selling to a group, or to a meeting (also a group) you want to wind up in rapport with almost everyone. This seemingly impossible task (different postures, representational systems, etc) can be conquered as follows:

1 Notice (in a group) which people are in rapport with whom. You will discover five or six clusters.

2 Note the person in each cluster who is paying the most attention. Continue to speak directly to these 'cluster leaders'.

3 Identify those clusters where leadership is weak (ie not paying much attention to you). Match them, get their representational systems through dialogue, and bring them on board.

4 Others in each cluster will follow.

5 Identify those few remaining 'stragglers' and appeal to them directly, making a special effort to match and have them gain ownership of what you are saying.

Similar processes can be used for meetings.

USING METAPHORS AND STRATEGIES

Metaphors and strategies are important for one-on-one situations. However, because of their very frequent usage in groups, we will discuss them here.

It is very common for people, when directly familiar with technical subject matter in the work place, to have a 'loaded gun' and be ready to object to what you have to say—sometimes, it seems, almost before you say it! People often have preconceived notions or biases. When these come up, we stop listening, and start rehearsing the objection or the 'point that we must absolutely raise' even before the speaker is done.

We cannot always control whether our listener is going to be a good listener. What we can do, however, is frame the subject matter in a way that will attract the interest of the listener and raise fewer objections. Verbal rapport, of course, is one way. Another is the use of *metaphor*.

Metaphors

A simplistic, useful way of describing a metaphor is as a story or analogy about something. This 'story' does not seem directly related to the subject matter at hand. It may seem to focus on, or discuss, the listener's hobby, or sport, or everyday personal life. The point is the analogy: the point the story makes, by analogy, is the same as the technical conversation or problem to be solved in the first place. The metaphor, or story, or analogy, raises fewer objections, and gives the listener ownership of the premise about to be mentioned in the ensuing technical discussion.

There are two key types of metaphors: general (sometimes called 'universal') and specific (sometimes called 'isomorphic'). Universal metaphors have the greatest chance of matching the broadest audience. However, like the digital communication style discussed earlier (which is a universal match of representation systems), they have only modest power. Isomorphic metaphors can be razor sharp and directed to people of a certain skill level or industry, and have much more power, like being richly V–A–K in speech predicates. Like those predicates, however, there is the risk of mismatch if not all of your audience understands the analogy. Good presenters use a mixture of both.

Your metaphors are best when they have a number of 'sub-analogies' or 'hooks' in them, which exactly parallel the situation you are trying to depict.

The best way of making the point is to use one here. I will construct a metaphor that shows the importance of matching before leading in speaking.

'It is important to match where your listener is, before leading them on to where you want them to be. If you mismatch, or lead too quickly, they will get lost, or disconnect from you, or crash into you, in a sense.

'Matching your listener before leading is just like a train. We all know a train is an engine, or locomotive, then a series of cars or boxcars, followed by the caboose (guard's van). You are the train's engine, and your listener or listeners are the rest of the cars. Let's start up the train, then uncouple the engine from the boxcars. The engine can speed up, and yet the boxcars will not follow. The engine can stop, and the boxcars will continue until they crash into the engine. The uncoupled engine can go up the hill, yet the boxcars will remain behind and fall backwards.

'To make sure that the rest of the train follows you, there are three steps. First, the engine and the train cars must be going at the same speed. Next, they have to be right next to one another. Finally, they have to be coupled. Now, when the engine speeds up or slows down, the cars follow. Wherever the engine goes, the cars go as well. If the engine selects a different parallel track, the cars go there also. If uncoupled, the cars would have gone their own way.

'And so it is with communication. You must be going the same speed and direction and purpose, be matched together, and linked, first! Then, and only then, can you lead the others to speed up, slow down, follow your direction, and go up the mountain with you'.

This comprehensive metaphor not only used a story line with a lot of 'hooks' (speed, linkage, tracks); it also used smaller metaphors of its own both in the original subject matter and the storyline itself (double metaphors such as crash, up the mountain, and so forth).

Strategies

In addition to using metaphors and verbal rapport, you can also 'calibrate' to your listener's thinking strategy. In addition to having a preferred system, if you pay attention, you will notice that your listener uses a certain sequence of systems to arrive at a decision.

You could ask him or her, for example, to tell you how they decided to select and implement a certain plan of action in the past. As they describe it, you may notice, for example, that they get a certain picture of alternatives; conduct an auditory mental dialogue weighing the alternatives; get a feeling about it, then come to a conclusion, visualising the result.

Now, in addition to calibrating to this system and prefacing it with metaphors, you might explain your suggested implementation in visual alternatives, describe the weighing of different options in auditory ways, and use kinesthetic (feeling) words to come to the conclusion you suggest, picturing the outcome. Notice how you are not only using metaphors to match; you are using predicates sequenced in the same way as your listeners'.

Remember, to you, the new learner, this may at first seem to be manipulation. However, it is a psychological fact that no one makes decisions, even under hypnosis, against their basic moral and ethical premises. Your listener's decision may be in your favour, or it may not. When you realise that most arguments and selling jobs are lost because the concept is not communicated clearly, you will realise the value of this communication technique. That is why so many good ideas in companies become lost in the woodwork. Good ideas, recognised as such by your listener, now have a much greater chance of acceptance and implementation.

Exercise: Practice metaphor

The following pages depict certain quality principles. You have seen some of these in Chapter 2, and some you have not. Perhaps you would like to get a group of team mates together. Each of you can take a page that you relate to, and construct a metaphor depicting the principle outlined on the page. Then, each of you can present your metaphor to other members of the group.

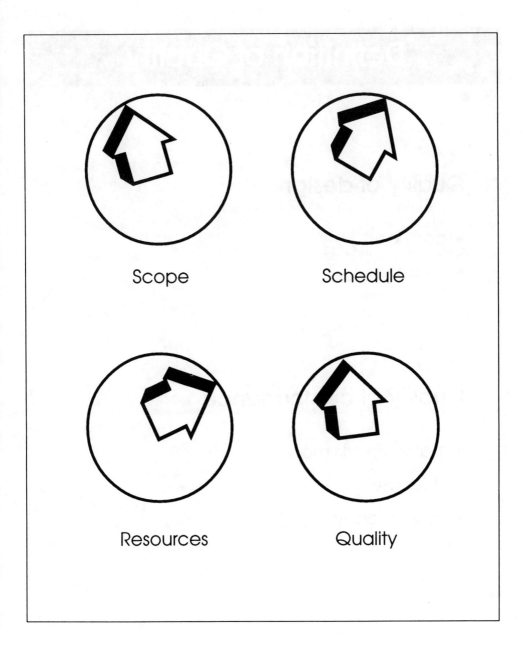

Scope

Schedule

Resources

Quality

Definition of Quality

Quality of design

- adds cost
- creative

Quality of conformance

- requirements met
- fit for use
- saves money

Definitions
Acceptable quality level: 99.9%

outcomes

18 aeroplanes crash daily

17,660 mail mix-ups hourly

3,700 bad drugs dispensed daily

10 dropped babies daily

$24.8 million mischarged hourly in banks

500 bad surgeries weekly

Quality concepts

3 main concepts

- management is responsible
- everyone is involved
- goal is to be defect-free

The Cost of Quality

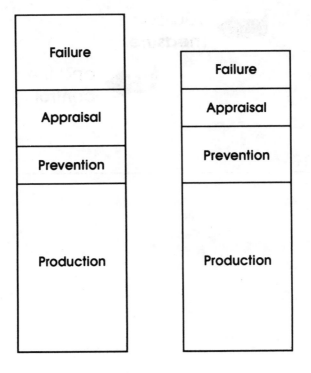

Failure is reduced when prevention is increased

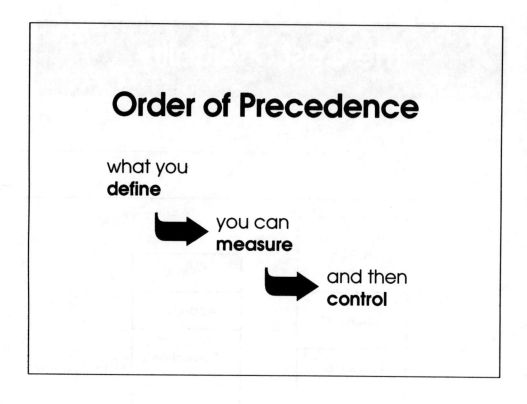

Order of Precedence

what you
define

you can
measure

and then
control

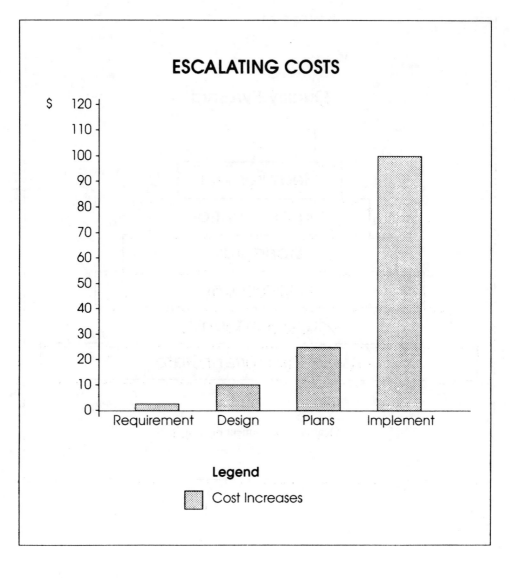

GOOD SALESMANSHIP

When you tie key elements of salesmanship to communicating effectively, working with groups, one on one, metaphors and strategies, you have true effectiveness. So, one way of packaging what you are 'selling' is to:

- create the need, if the need is unclear;
- get buy-in and acceptance and ownership;
- identify objections before they do;
- overcome those objections with thought-out solutions; and
- close the 'sale'.

Getting ownership is the key point. By using metaphors, you allow them to experience what you are saying rather than simply hearing you. If they experience it personally, it is much more powerful.

Visualising yourself as successful and having confidence helps enormously also.

I am indebted to a friend in Singapore, Allen Pathmarajah (former CEO of Great Eastern Life Insurance) for these seven steps, or stages, of relationship-based selling. You may find them helpful to calibrate where you are in the process with your customers.

- Suspect
- Prospect
- Customer
- Client
- Partner
- Advocate
- Friend

Exercise: Best sell

Pick a special topic directly applicable to your work area. This topic will be something that is important to emphasise or sell, yet which you have had very little luck with so far.

You are about to have two minutes, and two minutes only, to sell your point as if to the most senior, negative (toward this issue) individual in your organisation. Of course, someone else will be standing in for him or her as a role play. Give it your best shot, using all the techniques learned so far in this book.

Under simulated circumstances, some of you may want to practise this in front of an executive in a hostile environment (once you are skilled of course).

Take this time now to plan those all-important two minutes.

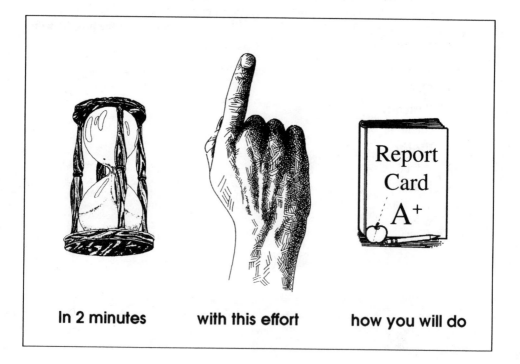

In 2 minutes   **with this effort**   **how you will do**

EFFECTIVE GROUPS—TEAM DYNAMICS

There are special considerations when interacting with more than two people: team dynamics. Probably the most important point is that there are many groups, yet few teams. True teams are rare, as we mentioned in Chapter 1.

Here are some of the characteristics that lead to a true team, and some of the dynamics that then occur:

- task/relationship
- group synergy
- ownership
- moderate conflict
- handling people
- stimulating others
- process, not content

Task/relationship

The balance between *task and relationship* is much misunderstood. As you can gather, virtually everything we discussed on rapport is a way to build relationships. Certainly, with any new team, building a relationship and a sense of trust among team members increases the degree of cooperation and sharing. More people will work with one another. Fewer hidden agendas will exist. What people do not understand is that even in established teams, some small degree of relationship building is needed.

Have you ever met with someone you know very well (perhaps even worked with extensively on the previous day) who started immediately to 'get down to business', to the details of the task at hand? If so, it may have been a little jarring. For many of you who are task-oriented, your task will be to build a relationship first! If you fit this category, your fear is probably that you won't get to the task at hand if you spend 'too much time' on building a relationship. My experience is that you cannot spend too much time on relationships—you do the job until it is done. Teams bonded in this way can work together at extraordinary speed. It is so extraordinary that the task time saved more than makes up for the time spent building the relationship. For the doubtful among you—try it and measure it!

Group synergy

Group synergy is the extent to which a team is more productive and has more wisdom than the best member of the team. Some people believe that the team strength is limited by the knowledge or ability of the 'best' person. Repeated studies show that team decisions (not group decisions) are stronger and better than the best member of the team—provided relationships are built properly beforehand, of course.

Ownership

Each member of a team must have a high degree of *ownership* of the process. This means they must be a 'stakeholder' in the activities. Some say that this means, 'What's in it for me?'; the answer to that question is very clear.

Moderate conflict

Contrary to common belief, extreme harmony of team members does not always give the best decisions. *Moderate conflict* helps team members to pose alternate points of view, resulting in better decisions. Sometimes extreme harmony results from fear of breaking rapport rather than true friendship; people fear that a dissenting view would be destructive. This is the reason that relationship building is so important. Strong relationships give teams 'resilience' to withstand the slings and arrows of dissent, without taking it personally.

Failure to consider the importance of moderate conflict has had damaging results. When people fear dissent, they say 'yes' when they mean 'no'. This is where the term 'Yes-man' comes from. It is widely held that in the Bay of Pigs invasion of Cuba ordered by USA President John F. Kennedy, many staff had reservations but didn't express them. The invasion was botched, of course, for some of the reasons that those people feared. It is also postulated that the USA Space Shuttle Challenger disaster, where the shuttle exploded shortly after take-off, was due to the non-acceptance of dissent. An engineer was very concerned that the rubber seals on the booster rocket were not certified for such a low temperature on that cold morning. He was effectively overruled, the launch proceeded anyway, and the rocket blew up—because the seals failed.

Handling people and stimulating others

Dissension can go too far. In any team, moderate dysfunctions exist. You may need to *handle overly expressive people* so everyone gets a chance. You may also need to *stimulate others* to share their views, just because they are somewhat quieter. (By the way, very often those that have been most silent have listened and been thinking more!)

Process, not content

As always with team facilitation, the *process* for any interaction governs how the *content* goes, and not the other way around. At least one, and preferably all team members, can be mentally 'watching' the team process as an observer (third position) as well as a participant.

DYSFUNCTIONAL BEHAVIOURS

Many of us have behaviours that, from time to time, prevent our teams from achieving their best. There are some team members (perhaps I can say group members) who seem to exhibit these characteristics consistently. It is these *dysfunctional behaviours* that we are referencing here. Examples (in metaphorical terms) are listed below and need little further explanation.

There are many facilitator training manuals that have complicated rules specifying what one can or cannot do, depending on the type of dysfunction. In my experience, few people are highly enough trained or fast enough on their feet to know just exactly what to do.

I have found that whenever a team member is exhibiting dysfunctional behaviour like one of those below, there is generally a fear there. You can take this fear from them so that they do not have to disrupt the meeting to get what they need. Most of us can discern the fear behind each of these behaviours. Use the second NLP position to determine what the facilitator would do to remove your fear, if you were them, then use that technique in your meeting. That's all there is to it!

Effective groups
dysfunctional behaviours

eager beaver

bulldog

dampener

acceptor

battler

chatterbox

rambler

reserved

daydreamer

griper

EFFECTIVE MEETINGS

Meetings don't have to be a waste of time. They can be more than a one-way information flow. Meetings that report on project status are an excellent way to share what has happened, and to decide what to do. To keep meetings on track, make an agenda, stick to it, and invite only those people who are an integral part of the process. One company I have worked with asks about meetings, 'Did you make a PAL for it? (Purpose, Agenda, Length)'. By the way, I like to cover urgent items first, and make sure the bulk of the time on the agenda is scheduled for important rather than urgent discussion items.

Organisational meetings are structural in nature. Unless it is a technical or problem-solving type meeting, its purpose is to take existing work and structure new work from it. As such, most of the work is done before and after meetings, not during them. So, if the agenda is disseminated in advance, it can call for task forces to do whatever pre-preparation or research is required. Then, during the meeting, the already-performed work can be examined and discussed. At these types of meetings, don't solve problems; identify them, assign them and move on.

One of the largest problems is how to structure unstructured time. While time for brainstorming happens primarily in problem-solving meetings, it can happen in other meetings as well. Put time for it on the agenda, and put it first since creative thought precedes rational thought. Book a time limit to put boundaries around it, and stick to it.

Late starts are a major time-waster—count the number of person hours that they waste. A 15 minute late start to a meeting with 12 people is a three person-hour delay! Many people try a number of creative approaches to this: locking doors at start time, starting anyway with most members absent, ending at the same time as planned regardless of the start time, holding meetings with no chairs, holding meetings at the end of the day so lateness goes after hours, and so on. The most effective technique I have seen is this: unless all scheduled attendees are at the meeting at exactly the start time, cancel the entire meeting and re-schedule it. This seems dramatic, yet it is very effective. This happens at most once or twice, so in the short run, it is prevention-based. The peer pressure to find out who did not show, and why, is so enormous that it doesn't happen again. Since people sometimes have unexpected travel schedules or illness, I suggest that every meeting person have an assigned person as a backup. That person must be empowered to make all decisions in the absentee's place, and must be fully prepared. Thus, there is never a reason why one person cannot be present for each area.

With some exceptions, I postpone the handout of any supporting material to my discussion (and use overheads instead) until the end of the meeting. This prevents unnecessary paper shuffling and rifling (and related daydreaming) while you are trying to lead or present.

Keep to the schedule in the agenda more often than not, and of course, have timely minutes describing both what happened and who is assigned to be responsible for what. I do not agree with 'politically sanitised' minutes that reflect what 'should' have taken place rather than what did take place. If an official 'party line' is required, make it separate.

Effective groups effective meetings

- **non-wasteful**
- **agenda**
- **selected members**
- **pre-preparation**
- **punctuality**
- **handouts**
- **keep to the agenda**
- **timely minutes**

PROBLEM-SOLVING STEPS

There are certain categories of meetings that are intended to solve problems or achieve related problem-solving tasks. Often, they are 'spin-offs' from regular meetings. Many team members are so proud of the productivity of these meetings, and dislike regular meetings so much, that they call them 'work groups'.

And yet, without a certain form or structure, it is unlikely that problems will actually be solved very well. The page at the end of this topic illustrates the eight steps to problem-solving.

You can group the first three points into the general category of 'brainstorming' or 'greenlighting'. You can group the next two into 'analysis', and the last three into 'roadblocks' or 'redlighting'. Walt Disney, of Disneyland and Disneyworld, called these three general categories dreamer, realist and critic. At a planning session attended by his engineers (called imagineers) he would often come in, unannounced, and be in any one of these modes, unpredictably. The idea was to have his people be fluent at all three major techniques (brainstorming, analysis and redlighting).

The reason for having a sequence is very important. If, in the middle of creative thought brainstorming, someone acts like a critic, brainstorming shuts down immediately. Creativity must continue until creativity is done, then analyse the options, then play 'devil's advocate' to make sure the solution is robust.

There is a chemical in the brain that is released slowly and accumulates during the brainstorming process. The amount released accelerates as ideas become more wild, crazy and humorous. This explains why ideas flow more quickly as people get 'warmed up'. Yet the flow of this chemical stops and creativity is shut down immediately with the first major criticism; the brainstorming mood then has to be recouped.

Let's have a look at the overall summary, then look at the steps in some detail.

Effective groups problem solving steps

1 define the problem

2 define solution criteria

3 brainstorming

4 analyse options (reduce list size)

5 weigh, then choose

6 list roadblocks

7 action steps

8 control, follow up

The dreamer stage

Defining the problem is a very much overlooked first step. Most declared 'problems' are really symptoms. You cannot solve problems well by attacking symptoms, because you are not going for the root cause. In many cases, finding the problem is the problem. My test: the *problem* is that issue for which, when found, a solution is apparent.

The criterion for the solution is that you can know in advance what attributes it will have, and know how you will know it when you see it. Otherwise, you could run right past the solution and not know that you have found it.

Brainstorming comes next. Most people go straight to this step, unfortunately, skipping the first two steps. This is the stage where you try to creatively come up with all possible solutions to the problem. Don't hesitate to put in crazy, humorous ideas—it 'juices' the creativity.

You can use these steps even in family situations. For example, let's say you are trying to figure out ways of sharing use of the telephone with your teenage daughter. This problem seems equally large no matter where I go! You and your family start to brainstorm. Well, you could bomb the telephone company, there would be no more phone service, and so you wouldn't have the problem any more. That indeed is a solution. Not a practical one, perhaps! Then you could go on to brainstorm more practical solutions, until you find the one that works best by following the rest of the steps.

There is even a method (structure), to make best use of brainstorming (the lack of structure!). Get a group of people together, and follow these three steps for brainstorming:

1 take some private time to record your individual ideas first;
2 take one new idea from each person while someone writes them down on an easel or paper;
3 keep up the pace. When everyone has had a turn, start at the first person again; if you are out of ideas, say 'Pass'. If you come up with a new idea not on paper, you can add it when it comes to your turn. When most people pass, then get ideas in any order, 'popcorn' style (you can't tell what kernel, or person, is going to pop next).

To practise this, take 60 seconds (set your timer) to record as many ways to use a paper clip as you can.

Individual Brainstorming List

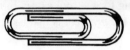

1
2
3
4
5
6
7
8
9
10
11
12
13
14
15
16
17
18
19
20

Now do steps 2 and 3.

The private time insures that the number of ideas does not depend upon one's spontaneity, or whether they are shy or extroverted. It will help to keep things moving and give everyone a chance if you take one idea from each person (rather than all ideas from one person). Keeping up the pace (a natural result of step 2) will prevent people from judging and acting as 'critic' to any of the ideas. Believe me, some of the ideas can be very easy to judge!

The realist stage

Steps 4 and 5 of the problem-solving steps are the analysis, or 'realist' stage. Of the perhaps 30 or 40 ideas, find some technique to reduce the size of the list to perhaps 10 or less. You can do this through discussion, voting, or any number of weighted voting schemes such as the nominal grouping technique. This popular technique has each person score each of the 30 to 40 items based on importance to them. The scoring is a priority, with '10' highest and '1' lowest. Adding all numbers for each person, for each of the ideas, gives a composite score. Sorting for the 10 highest scores reflects everyone's balanced opinions much better than a yes or no vote alone.

Once you have a small list, then open discussion is achieved. By weighing the advantages and disadvantages of each solution, the entire group chooses the best idea through consensus, not voting. Consensus means that, through adequate discussion, all points of view are heard and each person can live with the decisions made by the entire team. Voting creates winners and losers and breaks up teams; consensus is win-win and binds teams together.

The critic stage

Steps 6–8 of the problem-solving process take the best solution and 'redlight' or act as 'critic' to it. Sometimes the best solution is the hardest or most expensive to implement. It is occasionally necessary to overturn the best solution in favour of the second best, just because it is more achievable. The steps include listing all the barriers, assessing the action steps needed to overcome the barriers (which may be mini projects in themselves), and then controlling and following up.

The follow up is important. There is no direct evidence for knowing that the proposed solution, once implemented, actually solves the root cause. The solution might now work if you failed to properly identify the problem or ran right past the right solution because you didn't set solution criteria correctly. If not all roadblocks are seen or properly overcome, or you solved the wrong problem, the symptoms will still occur. You need to control the process so that you are assured that the result is effective.

EFFECTIVE STAFFING AND WORK

This last section in this chapter shows you how best to motivate your people and make them most effective: not by using motivational techniques but instead having them become self-motivating due to the work itself.

I happen to believe that you can't motivate people directly. What you can do is create an environment in which they motivate themselves. Do you know anyone with a low-quality hobby? Think about it! Motivation doesn't come from the 'boss' (since no boss is present) and if it is a hobby, it can't be the pay! It is that person's natural desire to be motivated.

You can, however, influence the structure of the work, the degree of initiative and the number of roadblocks, which greatly influences in turn a person's desire to be self-motivated.

Removing monkeys from your back as an anti-stress move, mentioned earlier in this book, not only improves your discretionary time, it also empowers your people and motivates them. Removing obstacles from their paths keeps this motivation alive. You can find out what motivates individuals and make sure they have more of that available to them.

One of the most effective ways of getting and keeping motivation is to structure the work effectively. Fred Herzberg developed a 'work effectiveness model' that is still effective today in describing what truly motivates people. It is not the pay; money is not a motivator at all in the long term, although its absence can be a demotivator. The only long-term motivator is the content of the work itself.

As a project manager, you have an opportunity to structure the work so that its content is rewarding. You can juggle who gets what pieces of work, or tasks, in such a way that this happens!

There are three things that influence the effectiveness of work this way. They are called the core job dimensions:

- the meaningfulness of the work itself (the task significance, skill variety, and task identity);
- the responsibility one feels for the outcome of the work; and
- the feedback one gets from the work itself, not from a person.

These dimensions have roughly equal weight.

The meaningfulness of the work is based on the significance of the task (the difference that the activity makes in the lives or work of other people); the variety of skills used, and how identifiable the work is as a single unit (how much of the entire job the person does). Police officers, firefighters, doctors, nurses, and airline pilots all have a high degree of task significance in their work. An entrepreneur or a one-person storekeeper has a great deal of skill variety, while an artist who completes an entire painting (conception, sketches, painting, framing, selling) has high task identity.

The personal responsibility one feels for the outcome of the work depends on one's involvement with it. Project managers feel a great deal of this personal responsibility.

Feedback is best when it comes from the work itself and not from other people. Sadly, most feedback from people is anecdotal and negative; or if it is positive, we think that they are up to something! The work doesn't care, and it doesn't have a personality, so most of us don't get mad at it. For example, a programmer gets consistent feedback from the work when source code compilations or execution testing reveals defects.

You can re-arrange the sequence and timing of work to vary the tasks, have people learn new things, and structure the system so it gives feedback by itself. Our temptation is to segment the work to make it more 'efficient'. Theoretical efficiency often robs work of interest, thus slowing down the people doing it to the extent that all 'efficiency' gains are lost.

Why do some sales representatives have territories? You could divide the work of five sales representatives up in two ways:

1 each salesman covers all geographic locations, and does one fifth of the work associated with each sale, like an assembly line, or
2 each salesperson covers one fifth of the geographic region (a territory) and does all of the work needed for each sale.

The second example is far more motivational and has a much higher degree of all work effectiveness factors.

12 Handling negotiations, conflict, and criticism

There are few among us who have not been (perhaps unfairly) criticised for the way we have handled or participated in a project. If you are a project manager, the very nature of your work often puts you in technical conflict with others in the organisation. Many projects are structured with 'matrix management' pulling one team member from each of a number of functional areas. This team may cut across many functions, perhaps seemingly at cross purposes to some of them. Or members of your team may be at cross purposes with one another.

Technical conflict, based on technology, is not uncommon and ordinary problem-solving techniques work here. What we are talking about is emotional conflict, which obviously absorbs the team in delaying activities and robs motivation.

There are also many times when we want to negotiate a structure in the best interest of pricing, timing, or the team. Properly handled, no conflict will result. However, conflict is sometimes a natural by-product of such negotiations and conflict resolution may be necessary.

As mentioned earlier, a moderate amount of conflict or dissension is desirable for best decision making. This section describes what to do when emotions are beyond that stage.

We will look at:

- conflict resolution and negotiation;
- thorough handling of emotional conflict; and
- handling criticism quickly.

CONFLICT RESOLUTION AND NEGOTIATION

When you take a negotiation position, it is important to ask for all of what you want, putting all of your requests on the table (however, not necessarily all of your plans or alternatives, at first). I believe in openness and honesty in negotiations, and realise that a negotiating partner may not behave that way. I don't believe in hidden agendas, and I also point out that there are those who may use against you some of what you share with them. This is, at times, a delicate balance. I find that if you keep your integrity, and are congruent (with beliefs and behaviours matching) then most people will want to join you on that level. In this way, you can also live with the outcome you yourself have asked for.

Negotiations often cause us to look at many aspects of our character. The ease with which we fall into conflict, rather than a negotiated settlement which is consensus-based, often depends on the strength, resilience, and integrity of our character.

My friend, Allen Pathmarajah of Singapore, shared with me seven components related to integrity, which he calls the '7 Cs'. You might find these useful in bringing a high quality person (you) to the negotiating table:

Elements of character —the 7 Cs

Conviction

Commitment

Competence

Courage

Character

Creativity

Caring

The QUALITY acronym for negotiating

My audio tape series *How to Achieve a Total Quality Life* has seven important character principles that will prove quite helpful in both self-examination and the leadership of character required for successful negotiating.

Let's look at these keys one by one.

Your long range objective in life, or purpose, might not be attainable in your lifetime. Even so, keeping this objective in mind will chart your course. Along the way, set specific achievable goals (mileposts) and feel free to modify them.

How you get there—the journey, or *quest*—is the difference that makes the difference.

In what ways have you been searching for your quest? In what ways could you be? Along the way, have you thought of your long-range objective or purpose? What is it? And what are some of your specific, achievable goals that are mileposts?

Understanding another's point of view means recognising another's perspective. Many perspectives are possible for the same situation by different people. To have understanding, get curious, not furious.

Recall some past discussions that made you angry, or furious. Had you been curious instead, what might you have learned?

Your personal *attitude* to continuous improvement means not settling for 'good enough' relationships. Everyone is doing the best they can. Are you? There are no failures, only feedback. Your 'mistakes' can be your greatest teacher.

Think of some specific ways that you judged someone (even yourself) for mistakes, or not doing the best they can. What could you have done instead?

Language is used, or misused, in many verbal and non-verbal ways. We mis-perceive other's meanings, and may inflict 'shoulds' and 'buts' on ourselves and others. Speak in positives! Reserve 'But' to make a positive counterpoint.

Where and when do you use the 'shoulds'? The 'buts'?

Walking what you talk, or practising what you preach, is *integrity*. It means doing what you believe, rather than deciding how to act.

As you work on your own congruence, recall what it was like behaving in a way that 'didn't fit' what you believe about yourself.

Do you have any examples and feelings about others who didn't walk the talk or act congruently?

The 7 keys to total quality

Q for **quest** for personal improvement and excellence

U for **understanding** of the other's point of view

A for your personal **attitude** towards improvement

L for **language** and its use in verbal and non-verbal ways

I for **integrity**, character and walking what you talk

T for **teamwork**, or working with others

Y for specific actions that **you** can take

Teamwork, or working well with others, is essential at home and at work. The world is filled with potential team members—we are not islands! Pulling together is more powerful than the best person pulling alone.

Identify how things went when true teamwork happened at home or at work.

What was it like when everyone had to fend for themselves, by comparison?

The specific actions *you* can take begin and end with *you*. *You* are the difference that makes the difference. *You* are Total Quality. You build skills going from Q ending with Y. Starting with Y, each of the keys supports each previous one, ending in the quest. Thus, quality ends, and begins, with *you*.

In the following figure, the outer circle is your personal life, fully enclosing the inner circle, your business life. The wavy line is the often unclear, and sometimes turbulent boundary between the 'yin' and 'yang' of life. The glass is half empty, and also half full. Your mistakes are either your greatest flaw or your greatest teacher. The choice is yours. What choice will you make? How will you balance the two?

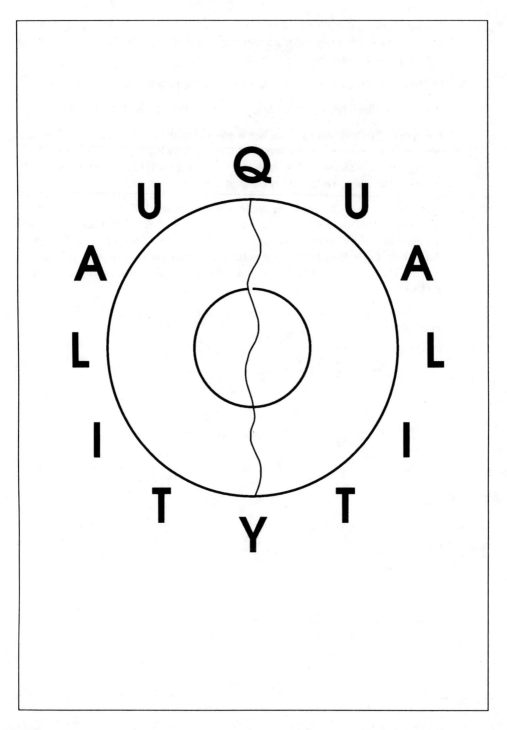

Basic negotiating skills

If you arm yourself with the 7 Cs and the QUALITY acronym, you are now ready to apply some basic negotiating skills. Here they are:

Getting started—conceptually

1   Identify outcomes, if known

2   Get information on the other's position

3   Be sure you can both decide

4   Agree on some basis for negotiation

5   Identify data, method, values

6   Use tools of rapport and NLP

It is important to be *outcome*-based rather than behaviour-based in any negotiation. Let go of how it should be done, or the form it should take, or how it should take place in a certain way. You are adding to flexibility when you do this. Usually, at a higher level, you want to accomplish a certain overall thing. Remember the NLP presupposition that people with the most flexibility have the most choices— you want to create an infinity of choices for yourself!

Getting information on each other's positions means not batting down what the other says until you have heard it all. Only without fear can you each express 100% of what you would like and put it on the table. This does not mean that you are going to get it. Rather, you are putting it all up for discussion, and listening to all of it.

Be sure you are both in a position to *decide* the outcomes of the negotiation. You must both be empowered to have the flexibility to adapt. Get this empowerment from your company before you start. Find out what you can and cannot compromise; be clear about that up front.

Especially if you are stuck in a rut, it is important to agree on some *basis* for negotiation. This means find a place on which you do agree, even in a field surrounded by disagreement. Logical levels helps here, but more on that later. People who 'agree to disagree' are actually finding common ground!

Frequently during a negotiation, clarity can occur if you find the context surrounding the disagreement. Then, you can usually negotiate in that particular arena:

- data: the issue surrounds elements of fact, for which data are available. Get the needed data, compare and resolve.
- method: the issue is over the way something is to be accomplished (the verb, the process) not the desired outcome itself (the noun, the product). Be flexible and entertain alternative verbs to get to the same noun.
- values: the issue relates to the values or beliefs of each of you and the fact that they may be in conflict. Search higher for what is in common, then find those values and beliefs that you agree upon.

Here are some golden rules that will help you during the discussion.

Be concerned about:

- validating the other's position

- avoiding putdowns

- labelling questions and suggestions first

- being flexible

- citing reasons, then proposing

- matching feelings

- emphasising agreement

- moving agreement into implementation

Most of the basic skill sets to be used are now familiar to you (see the list below). *Probing vagueness* will be discussed more in Chapter 14, with more on *logical levels* below. Two new areas are *demonstrated understanding*, and *questioning without interrogation*.

Demonstrated understanding is a method for matching a person, especially when undergoing conflict. Too often, we address the content of the issue, when in fact the person is either just venting or wants to be heard and acknowledged emotionally. This is a very powerful point.

To match emotionally, you can use an introductory phrase appropriate to the representational (V, A, K) system of the one who is venting, followed by an emotional match. Occasionally, you may need your intuition to guide you, coupled by second position. For example:

Venter   It is ridiculous to try and *get* my boss to *listen* to me on this issue.

You   It *sounds* like it frustrates you to *get* your boss in your corner.

Notice you are not agreeing with them, advising them, or asking questions. In short, you are providing no new information—just an emotional match.

Even in the face of a direct question, or when asked advice, I check out the tone of the request. If the tone is ordinary, I will answer the question or brainstorm with them. If they are emotionally charged, they need to be matched at the emotional level first. Sometimes I will do nothing other than emotional matches with no data provided, and very often they will solve the problem for themselves. Has this ever happened to you? A good friend just vents, you just listen and perhaps match, they solve their own problem, then thank you very much for giving them the solution!

At other, somewhat less charged, times, I will preface with demonstrated understanding, then follow with the advice or answer that is asked for.

Sometimes a person feels put on the spot unless we can *question without interrogation*. A question that sounds like it has a question mark at the end of the sentence can sometimes sound like an interrogation. In sensitive situations, you can ask a question without asking a question! How? By making a statement, that invites an answer, rather than probes for it. You still get the answer, and the other person does not feel like they are at the police station.

Good methods for doing this are to use introductory phrases such as 'I wonder if...' or 'I'm curious to know what...' or 'I'm puzzled about...', to name a few. Following the phrase, make a statement that would have been a question, if it had words like 'Do you...' at the front of it.

For example:

Old way   Did you stop by the store to get some milk today?

New way   I wonder if you stopped by the store to get some milk today.

I wonder if you noticed the difference between the old way and the new way.

(Could I have said, 'Did you notice…'!!?!)

The basic skill sets, and especially the two discussed above, work especially well during conflict as well as negotiation, and are excellent for families too.

I wonder if you agree.

Basic skills to use

- Build rapport

- Put relationship before task

- Probe vagueness

- Demonstrate understanding

- Question without interrogation

- Use logical levels

- Realise multiple models of the world

Sometimes, the other party has an agenda that prevents proper negotiation and leads to conflict. Here is a checklist of possible blocks to cooperation that you might want to look out for.

Cooperation blocks

- Differing goals/objectives
- Lack of interest
- It can't be done
- It can be done better outside the group
- Non-acceptance of responsibility
- Misunderstanding
- Lack of clarity of goals
- Unfairness, frustration, confusion
- Withdrawal
- Resentment
- Transgression against group
- Unnecessary judgements
- Misidentification of group member
- Pity-party

- Differing assumptions
- View that other is unethical
- Results are not worth the time
- Clashing styles
- Non-interest in the group
- Activity not in job description
- Misinformation
- Pain, loss, fear
- General apathy
- Anger
- Hostility
- Unnecessary force
- Unnecessary hiding
- Elitism
- Success destroys other goals

More on logical levels

Earlier in this book, we showed how the logical levels concept was useful for matching one on one. We suggested then that it was a great tool for resolving conflict. Remember, if the discussion sounds like a personality clash, check for mismatching V, A, or K predicates. If you notice that you honour the person, yet are stuck in conflict, you are in all likelihood at mismatched logical levels. Remember that you can firstly assess whether you are matched, then match yourselves, and finally move upward on the pyramid to the spot where you agree.

Picture an upside-down tree suspended in mid-air. All twigs, branches and boughs join at the trunk where they are in common (in this metaphor, this is the point where you can both agree). For all you know, you may match at the branch or the bough level before you get to the trunk. Moving down the levels slowly, you can work your way along the same bough, branch and twig. It may not be the same twig you started on, yet it will be one compatible with the outcome. Here is a diagram.

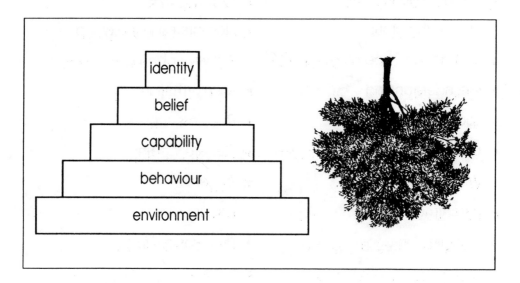

How do we apply these principles? The concept of proper and improper matching of logical levels can be depicted in the following example. It is between an information systems (IS) auditor and an information systems (IS) professional in a bank. Suppose that the auditor is stating a concern with the software (on the 'behaviour' logical level) to an IS professional, as follows:

ISP You do not know how hard I have worked on this project, and don't appreciate the pressures I am under. My work is valuable and I do a good job. How can you know it as well as I do? I am a valuable programmer. You can't understand my situation. [Identity level]

Auditor But you must understand that the security aspects of coding in this section do not address the company concerns. [Behaviour level response]

What just happened? The IS professional gets furious, and the auditor is frustrated. The IS professional clearly associates his behaviour (the work) with his identity and self-worth. Rather than match the programmer's desired identity, the auditor responds with behaviour.

Let's replay this conversation, first matching the programmer at the identity level, then moving through the logical levels to behaviour:

ISP You do not know how hard I have worked on this project, and don't appreciate the pressures I am under. My work is valuable, and I do a good job. How can you know it as well as I do? I am a valuable programmer. You can't understand my situation. [Identity]

Auditor I understand these pressures. I have seen the work you have done, and it is excellent. You have done a lot of great work for the corporation, and are a valuable member of the team. [Identity]

ISP Well, I don't know the value of the encryption auditing concern. It seems to me that the approach I am using is sufficient. [Belief]

Auditor Because of the fact that we have open communication lines, sending this data in the clear would subject our company assets to tremendous exposure and fraudulent alteration. By encrypting the transmitted data, we greatly safeguard our company assets, without reducing performance. Do you remember the incident last year when the computer hacker transferred all those funds to his personal account? [Belief]

ISP I sure do. I'm not sure I am able to do this. How can I accomplish this encryption? [Capability]

Auditor By attending our special class, and reading this manual I give you now, you will learn everything you need to know. [Capability]

ISP What specific method can I use, and what can be done? [Behaviour]

Auditor   I would recommend using algorithm two on page 14. [Behaviour] This addresses our auditing and security concerns without sacrificing performance, so you won't be criticised for inefficient programs. [Identity rematch] If you believe that this is important [Belief rematch], and that you understand the algorithm [Capability rematch], then you will be able to accomplish it. [Behaviour]

ISP   Suppose my boss tells me that there is not enough time or budget for it, and that it won't work here? [Environment]

Auditor   I would be glad to explain the situation, and to find a way of spending this time, ultimately saving schedules and budgets greater than the current plan. Failure of security would, after all, kill the current schedule and budget with massive rework. [Description of matching supervisor's belief system] We can both show him how it can work here, and to his benefit. [Environment]

In this comprehensive example, notice the auditor's attention to:

- locating the present state of the IS professional (identity) rather than the intended initial state of the auditor (behaviour and behaviour change);
- truthfully matching the IS professional at that level, validating identity without compromising behaviour;
- working down the logical levels and getting agreement at each level, before tackling the key issue; and
- making sure environment issues are addressed.

THOROUGH HANDLING OF EMOTIONAL CONFLICT

If you and a team mate are in conflict emotionally, or you as a project manager notice your team mates are in conflict, this process model will work well to resolve it:

1 Have each party discharge the anger physically (brisk walking, working out, going into the woods and screaming).
2 Unload it onto a third party (a party not involved in the conflict).

   At this stage, the anger or upset is 'cleaned up' to the extent that it has a chance of being worked on constructively. Sometimes, by sharing the upset with an uninvolved person, the one who is upset can see how they have contributed to the conflict.

3 Put it on the table, face to face (share your truth, one at a time, about how you feel and think while the other listens without interruption).
4 Negotiate lists of what you want the other person to do more of or less of (swap lists).

Remember, your truth may not be *the* truth in the world. Listening without interruption allows them to be completely heard, maybe for the first time. You can believe, however, that whatever you hear is very true for them. When exchanging lists, you are not required to do what is asked. You can also volunteer what you personally would be willing to do, even if not asked, as an alternative. By actually doing what you have agreed, you will build up trust and goodwill.

HANDLING CRITICISM QUICKLY

Sometimes, even the best laid plans and processes go awry when we suddenly become the target of criticism, real or perceived. We do our best to match systems, use metaphors, and identify strategies, and suddenly a curve is thrown at us, and we lose it. What do we do?

First, there are ways of presenting things so that they lead to less argument and criticism in the first place. Second, we must be prepared to deal with objections, criticism or attack when it does come. This section deals with the first. The exercise that follows deals with the second.

In any computer system, software, or hardware, the component with the greatest number of options and most flexibility will usually have the greatest use and effect. It is the same with people. You can only communicate by constant, resourceful, attentive flexibility.

Many of us think of conflict as akin to verbal boxing. You may pound through your arguments until you get the changed behaviour you want, but this approach is not usually successful. The issue is not to win or lose. In fact, it is not even necessary to enter, or remain on, the battlefield!

A much more elegant and effective model is that of the oriental martial arts like aikido. There, the goal is not to overcome force but instead to redirect it; not to meet force with force, instead to *align* yourself with the force directed at you, and guide it in a new direction. In a sense, this is like matching and leading discussed earlier.

The 'Aikido of Politics' is similar. A good communicator:

- is flexible and resourceful enough to sense the creation of resistance, instead of opposing;
- finds points of agreement within the disagreement;
- aligns herself with those points; and
- redirects communication in a way that she wants it to go.

In addition, there are certain 'land mines' in language that can trigger argumentative responses in others, send wrong messages to the subconscious, or deflate our self-worth and value. One example is stating things in negatives, rather than positives: the subconscious hears the sentence with the 'don't' removed and does the opposite of the intended behaviour, eg 'Don't drink and drive' (compare with 'Drive sober').

Some words and phrasings need to be avoided; alternatives can be found:

- use '*and*' rather than '*but*'; '*but*' raises defences;
- use '*when*' more often than '*if*'; it is more affirming and leaves fewer ways out;
- use accenting within the sentence to make your point. For example, emphasise *you* within a sentence containing compliments, as '*You* did a nice job'. Emphasise the action with objectives, such as. 'What do you *think*?'
- focus more heavily on process rather than content. Keep adding to your arguments, rather than removing from theirs. During times of pressure, when attacked, we often are defensive, focusing more on content. Note, however, it is usually the process that has gone wrong leading to this in the first place;
- if you're having difficulty doing something, say (and think), 'I can't do this *well yet*', rather than 'I can't do this'. Better still, say: 'I can do this part well now'.

The rules of 'engagement' are:

- First, be comfortable and confident about yourself (see next exercise).
- Find an agreement frame and build on it.
- Turn resistance into assistance.
- Do a 'pattern interrupt'.
- Use '*and*' to your advantage, and match.

Examples of the right way are:

- 'I appreciate your ... *and* see (feel, sense, hear, etc.) how it can be even more effective by doing (your idea).'
- 'I respect the ... *and* ...'
- 'I agree with ... *and* ...'

The wrong way:

- 'I understand your point about this, *BUT*... [notice your own reaction] ...this is the way we may do it instead.

The right way:

- 'I appreciate your point about this, and I agree with your thoughts on items one and two. *In addition*, I feel that your plan can be made even more effective if we add these additional concepts we discussed earlier'. [Note ownership assigned to listener.]

Is communication like this really necessary?

The Power of

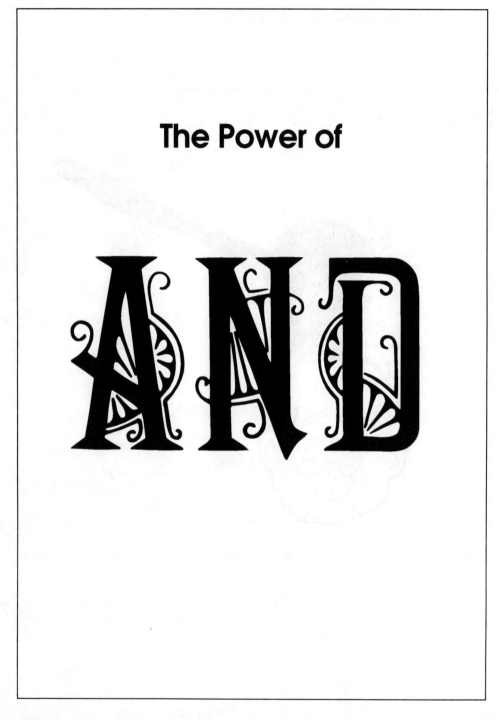

Criticism deflection technique

The technique is called 'Get curious, not furious'. It is based on the fact that for another to 'do' anger or criticism, they must be working externally rather than internally. Anger is the desire to make someone feel guilty. If you are angry or critical of yourself, it is the desire to make yourself feel guilty. That is the reason anger or criticism is external and not internal.

The following aikido technique gets that person to go internal, to answer a question you have posed to them. It is impossible to be both internal, thinking of the answer to a question, and external, trying to do damage, at the same time. It is an NLP impossibility.

Therefore, 'get curious, not furious' or for some of us, 'get curious, not defensive' means this: if you ask a question of your attacker, rather than get angry or defensive, their anger will quickly subside. It has to be a real question, because you really want to know, not something fabricated.

A wrong example is: 'Well, why do you think I would do something like that?' (not a real question, but a counter-attack instead)

A right example is: 'Wow, I didn't know it affected you like that. I am curious to know how I contributed to this problem'.

Two things happen when you ask questions: you quickly diffuse the anger, and you get information to the perceived way in which you might be 'guilty'. After all, if you did indeed contribute to the problem, you really want to know that. Even if you are convinced you did not, you still want to know why they think you are responsible. Notice in this inflamed situation, a non-interrogation 'question' (without questioning) was used.

The first time that I remember using this was when I was working for a contractor, as a subcontractor. I must have said something really off base, because she threatened to take me to court, file a lawsuit, and more. I no longer remember what the misunderstanding was (really!) because I have released it. However, I remember very distinctly the dynamic. She got so angry that she hung up the phone, in the middle of her own sentence, while she was talking! Try and picture that!

Well! I took a moment to breathe, and waited about 30 seconds, and decided I would be the one to call her back. By applying this technique, literally within 15–20 seconds we were both laughing and joking, and the issue was no longer at hand.

Some of you may have difficulty in remembering to use the skills, during this period of turmoil. We are sometimes not at our best when being attacked. If necessary, mentally 'jump' into observer (third) position and watch the two of you participate. You will not feel emotionally threatened from this position. If 'you need time, you can always pause. You do not have to give an instant response. If you need an excuse, then you can say something like, 'Just a moment, you made an interesting point. Let me ponder it for just a moment or two'.

Giving feedback instead of criticism

It is important not to be the one against whom others have to use these techniques! So how can we avoid being 'guilty' of criticising others?

I don't happen to think there is any such thing as 'constructive criticism': it is an oxymoron! All people hear is the critique; few treat it as constructive. There is such a thing as constructive feedback, however. The difference is this: criticism is negative and often attacks; feedback is positive.

The 'but' and 'and' example above is an example of feedback rather than criticism. Don't use the 'sandwich' technique (praise, followed by critique, followed by praise). Start thinking in terms that the Malcolm Baldrige National Quality Award folk used it: strengths, and areas for improvement, rather than strengths and weaknesses.

Share with your people what they do right. Share with them what they could do to make it even better. Avoid rights and wrongs.

For example:

Old   Your work in projects is really great, *BUT* your estimating job is totally lousy.

New   Your work in projects is really great, *AND* as you improve your estimating skills, it will be even better.

4 What they don't teach you in project management school

There are many fine texts and courses on the traditional aspects of project management. It is not the aim of this book to duplicate those efforts. Instead, we will focus on the most misunderstood portions of these traditional areas. A common shortcoming that I have seen both in my own training and in many texts, is that theory and practice differ. I have witnessed many others' frustrations at the fact that the real world differs from what was learned in the classroom!

This section mainly focuses on the differences between theory and practice—what they don't teach you in project management school. We will tacitly assume that you are quite familiar with the traditional concepts:

- size and scope of a project;
- work breakdown structures;
- estimation of tasks;
- automated tools;
- costing and funding;

- overall objectives;
- resource allocation;
- scheduling (PERT, CPM) and charting (GANTT) tasks;
- project control techniques.

We spent some time in Chapter 1 giving a brief orientation to these terms. Here and there, where required to illustrate the difference between theory and practice, we will briefly summarise some of these concepts first. We invite your attention to any of the texts and courses on these traditional aspects before proceeding with this chapter, as you see fit.

13 A fresh look at 'plan, organise, and control'

SEQUENCE OF PLANNING: THEORY VERSUS REALITY

One textbook approach to planning a project is:

1 Identify project overall objectives.
2
3 Define the work effort (work breakdown structure).
4
5 Estimate the work effort.
6 Select resources.
7 Develop the schedule.
8 Estimate costs.
9 Secure approval and funding.

Two things to note: first, this is a normal 'left to right' approach where the schedule and budget depend on the calculated work effort, as perhaps we were all taught. Second, notice the two missing steps.

We are going to fill in the missing steps in a moment. Note that even with all nine steps present, the textbooks say to plan a project in this order. In the real world, the majority of the time, it may be our boss that dictates steps 9, 8 and perhaps 7, forcing us to work backwards. What do we do? Do we abandon the left-right approach in favour of the right-left approach? Do we do both? Do we quit in frustration? Do we declare our boss and all managers to be idiots? Or do they have a point? What do we do?

First things first. Let's rewrite the nine steps above and fill in the two missing steps:

1 Identify project overall objectives.
2 *List the assumptions.*
3 Define the work effort (work breakdown structure).

4 *Define the tasks and products in detail.*

5 Estimate the work effort.

6 Select resources.

7 Develop the schedule.

8 Estimate costs.

9 Secure approval and funding.

Now, to be fair, there are a number of traditional project management texts that say something about steps 2 and 4. The important point is that these are the two most commonly forgotten steps.

Most people get a grasp of the overall project objectives. Step 2 says to actually *write down* the assumptions you are making with the work (and actually, at any time in the future, such as assumptions surrounding estimates). While many of us note, see or make certain assumptions, we seldom log them, and can easily forget them until they surprise us later. Not everyone has the same idea of assumptions as you. Your assumptions may include ideal models of the world, or tacit expectation that everything will go as planned. They could also be more pragmatic and realistic, with assumptions like these illustrations (far from a complete list):

- What am I assuming about project team stability? Have I considered the impact of a team member quitting?
- What about a person being pulled off a project to work on another? What if my team member is delayed on a prior project and can't start this one on time?
- Have I considered what would happen if prior phases are not ready? What if a supplier does not deliver on time?

So, not only do you look for what happens if things do not go as planned, you list your tacit assumptions that take place with the planning process. They may take forms like:

- I tacitly assume that the classroom training needed by my team for this task will have been accomplished on time and that the learning will have taken effect.
- I tacitly assume that my boss will not accelerate the schedule to earlier than the following date: _____ .
- I tacitly assume that the elements of task A and task B are exactly these _____ , and that the requirements will not change by more than 10% in this area over the life of the project.

This does not mean that these things will happen: it means that the assumptions form the basis for controls later on. When in front of you and reviewed frequently, they can call attention to 'looming disasters' before they actually occur.

I recommend brainstorming activities with the entire team to first formulate, then later update, the comprehensive list of assumptions. This will minimise the chance that something will escape your view. It is not usually a wrong estimate, instead it is usually the things we forgot to estimate or consider that get us in trouble.

Now let's look at step 4. Step 3 is to write down the titles of the tasks, having broken them down into smaller hierarchical steps. Step 4, often forgotten, is to write a detailed paragraph narrative of what we mean by that task. Why do this?

- We fail to consider that what we mean by a detailed task may be different from that assumed by our team members, customer or supplier.

- Expanding the title into a paragraph shows us unintentional, accidental overlap of work breakdown structure contents with other tasks. They are supposed to be, as mathematicians would say, 'mutually exclusive and collectively exhaustive'.

- Lack of agreed-upon knowledge of task contents leads to apparent 'scope creep' or 'changing requirements,' which are not really either one. We often blame customers for this. In reality, ill-defined tasks seem as if they grow when their unchanged definition becomes clear.

Now that we have looked at the missing steps, we can say a little bit about the prescribed order. In my experience, the numbered order is the correct, most prevention-based and efficient way to plan a project.

Some judgement calls occur around costing and people allocation. Sometimes, people are planned for you, or their selection occurs before the work breakdown schedule is defined. Costing depends on both schedule and people. Often, estimates depend upon which people do the tasks. So naturally, some iteration or resequencing is sometimes required. Given a 'tie', I generally prefer to allocate people after the tasks. Most people agree that the work needs to be broken down, estimated, and then scheduled.

To answer the bigger question: what happens when schedule, budget, and people are planned for me? Do I chuck the whole process?

No!

In fact, only by doing left-right planning, can we assess the impact of right-left (imposed) planning. We must in fact do both. No, our managers are not idiots! In Chapter 1, we illustrated why such a scenario can be reasonable (the trade show example). Present alternatives to your management, not ultimatums.

WORK BREAKDOWN, ESTIMATING, AND SCHEDULING

I have included some worksheets to make your planning process easier. One key worksheet is the 'process map', which contains some important new techniques.

First, some words on work breakdown structures. For large projects, resources can be broken down in the same way as smaller projects.

The aim of dissecting a large project objective into smaller chunks or tasks is principally this: the sum of a series of small guesses for estimates is generally more accurate than one large guess. Also, it is not the error in the estimate that gets us in trouble, it is the things we failed to include in our estimate. Breaking down the work makes it easier to estimate, to assign correct resources, to plan what must be consecutive and what can be in parallel, and to draw attention to forgotten details.

Generally, we break down into various levels. At level 1 is the whole project. Level 2 might be its four or five phases. Level 3 might be the content, or sub-project, of each phase, and level 4 would be the tasks within each sub-project, for example. At each new, more detailed level, we wish to be sure that nothing is left out (mutually exclusive and collectively exhaustive). Mentally, the trick that I use is this: when forming level 2 from level 1, for example, I mentally think of the unwritten level 3 items contained in each level 2 block. This ensures I have left nothing out, nor do I have overlap. Most importantly, I get brainstormed assistance from my team members to ensure I have all possible items. Remember I already got that brainstorming assistance in the assumptions list.

As mentioned in the step 1–9 descriptions in the prior section, I make sure, at the lowest level, to write detailed task descriptions when I am done (step 4 of 9).

Some worksheets that you might find helpful are given on pages 194–196.

Estimating

Tasks must be broken down to be estimated. Unfortunately, there are times when your boss wants to know the entire estimate and schedule for the whole project, and perhaps even resources and budget, before you have done this activity. That may be unfair, yet it is real life.

We have some techniques to help you with this, coupled with notes for scheduling (see page 197). Some of you may find this valuable enough to post as a process script. It covers most of the planning stage pieces in a new and realistic way to be handy as a reference. The worksheet is explained below.

Brainstorming List

List of elements of work breakdown structure

_____

_____

_____

_____

_____

_____

_____

_____

_____

_____

_____

_____

_____

_____

_____

_____

_____

_____

_____

Brainstorming List

List of unexpected events for estimating
(Has your estimate considered these things?)

_____

_____

_____

_____

_____

_____

_____

_____

_____

_____

_____

_____

_____

_____

_____

_____

_____

_____

Brainstorming List

What stands in your way of getting the job done?

What are the issues?	What can I do about it?

Process map for estimating

Gross estimate computation

- intuition times adjustment factor A
- recompute A over time = actual / estimated

Identify all the pieces (work breakdown structure)

- hierarchical pieces
- one person week per piece maximum
- must include deliverables in milestones

Correct amount of padding

- % of non-project time (actual history)
- unexpected events (has estimate considered them?)
- % of time for other projects (actual history)
- multiply by factor B
  done overall; recompute B over time = actual / estimated

Schedule the work

- schedules include critical path map—map the paths
- note the paths that are critical as anti-stress move

Budget the work based on project and elapsed time

- report to management the alternatives, not ultimatums
- identify risks
- expect 20% or more variance until after the detailed design

Control your progress

- keep good records and track milestone actual / estimated
- use non-critical path time to make up
- report status and re-estimate and schedule promptly
- use good time management techniques during the project

The first section of this worksheet, the *gross estimate computation*, comes first because it addresses the fact that your boss is going to ask you for the final estimate for the whole project. He will give you 10 minutes to do it, and you have no data yet on which to base it. Unfair? Yes! Can you estimate this more accurately than before? Of course!

My research has revealed that once you have been in the field for three years or more, you have a pretty good intuition of how long a project takes. The trouble is that your estimate is frequently biased on the long or short side (usually the short side). This is because we are often too optimistic about unexpected contingencies. The interesting thing is that although your estimated figure is off, the amount by which it is off is nearly a constant.

You should keep a log of your gross estimates (overall, unfair estimates of an entire project's time and cost) together with a history of the actual completion dates and costs. Remember, the weather forecast may be inaccurate; the weather report is 100% right. You will notice a trend, or factor (or multiplier) based on a ratio of actual/estimated. If you take your 'guess' and multiply it by this factor, then you are likely to be close to reality. Note that this overall estimate may not 'feel right'.

Now you can go ahead and do the planning as normal, by *identifying all the pieces* in the hierarchical ways we described. A good rule of thumb for medium-sized projects (six people, six to eighteen calendar months) is to shoot for a work breakdown structure of one person-week per task, and to make sure that you have actual, tangible deliverables at the end of those tasks if possible.

It is not that people lie; it is simply a fact that strange things happen if we call a 20 week activity a single 'task'. If we have not followed the techniques to avoid inducing fear in our team members, then it is hard to tell when this task is done, or how 'done' it is. Many team members simply cannot tell. They then revert to the calendar, noting it is 14 weeks into the 20 week schedule, and say, 'well, it is 14/20... I mean, 7/10 done'. Only when it nears week 20 do they sometimes come to us and say, 'Well, I ran into trouble, I need another 20 weeks'! I call this the 'fence post' analogy.

If you structure work as a deliverable product, either it is done or it is not. The intermediate product can be looked at and can be confirmed that it is done. It is not so much that we don't trust our people (remember, trust and empowerment are important): it is now a fact that the people themselves can tell if the product is done.

I pick a one week interval (which you may need to change) because on average, if you have weekly status meetings, each person has completed one new deliverable each week. Projects seldom go longer than a week before we note that they are in trouble—when we still have time to do something about it.

Occasionally, it is necessary to construct a deliverable in the milestone that might otherwise not be there. This can take some added effort. Generally speaking, the added effort is worth it compared to the cost of seeing a major problem too late. In fact, this is the major reason that software methodologies have deliverables. Even if the intermediate deliverable is not part of the final product, it is a clear indicator that the particular phase is done.

The *correct amount of padding* is another way of building in proper amounts of contingency time based on assumptions. By padding, we do not mean slack, or spare time. This is a calculated figure which, when done, will represent the actual expected completion time of tasks in the long run. Notice it is a composite of non-project time (fully applied, most people spend only 65–70% of their time applied on task), unexpected events, and time shared with other projects. Therefore, a person with two projects equally divided will spend 35% of their calendar day time on them, not 50%. Actual records should be kept by individuals so this can be calculated. A good source is the time log used in time management in Chapter 3.

Now, this is interesting. Even with proper consideration of outside factors, 'hope often springs eternal' with the estimation of individual tasks. My research once again shows that people guess wrong, yet by the same amounts as a ratio. Note that the multiplying factor for this particular ratio, factor B, is a different multiplier to factor A (used for the gross estimate of the entire project overall). Therefore, six sets of total records are needed for safekeeping by the team members (never by the project manager). You can require that people have them; never insist on seeing them or picking these factors for them.

1 % non-project time, actual
2 % of time for other projects, actual
3 Gross estimate guess
4 Gross estimate actual
5 Detailed estimate guess
6 Detailed estimate actual

There is a great deal in the industry, especially the software industry, about how to estimate the programming time for software based on number of function points, number of files, and other factors. The trouble with all of these algorithms is that some people can be 50 times more productive than other team members. You can, however, use such computations to compare your own past work to new, future work. Once again, the ratio of times for these estimation techniques is not bad, especially if you have had no experience with the new work. The only way to be sure you are scaling the time it takes to your own experience is to use factors A and B as explained.

The people doing the work should also do the estimates. A lousy estimate formed by the doer is much better than an excellent estimate formulated by the project manager. Why? Because a lousy estimate that is owned will be corrected, and an excellent one that is not owned will not necessarily be followed.

Scheduling

Work can be *scheduled* using PERT (Program Evaluation and Review Technique), CPM (Critical Path Method) or similar techniques. Note that you usually have to know the tasks, the estimates of task time, and the people who will be doing the task. An estimate says how many person-weeks a task takes; a schedule says by what time on the calendar it will be done. This considers a variety of factors. Some tasks can run concurrently with others, others must sequentially follow one another. When this piece is all done, there is generally one path through this 'network' that prescribes the overall time for completion, called the *critical path*. It is critical because any delay on this path delays the entire project. Conversely, delays on other paths may use up valuable spare time or *slack* time, yet the project will not be delayed.

Some key things follow about scheduling networks and critical paths that are not always mentioned in 'project management school'.

One of the purposes for drawing a network is that it shows you what to worry about. Without such a diagram, a project manager might be tempted to look at everything. With such a diagram, you can put most of your efforts into the things that matter, on the critical path. This gives you only one major thing to concentrate on for control and follow up at any given time.

Also, it shows you where you need to put your best people (on the critical path) and your trainees or new hires (on other paths). You can also use the slack time off the critical path to borrow resources to 'finance' the critical path should it become late, without delaying the project. You can also minimise the cost of resources by 'borrowing' from the non-critical paths, and therefore avoid the greater expense of hiring outside contract help.

Most importantly, a scheduling network shows you what you need to accelerate in the event that the boss picks a date sooner than the network calculates. We do not have to rush everything—we only need to 'crash' those tasks on the critical path, and we can calculate the added costs. These added costs may make sense, to gain strategic market advantage, or to make (rather than miss) a trade show. The cost of missing a market window may be far higher in revenue than the increase in project cost due to crashing, high as it may be. In any event, cost-revenue curves can be calculated to find the optimum balance point. It is these alternatives that you should present to management, not ultimatums. This gives management choices. See, management folk are not idiots after all!

Clearly, this is why you need to work 'left–right' (steps 1–9) as well as 'right–left' (steps 9–1), because otherwise you would not know what schedule network paths to accelerate to meet management objectives.

Of course, risks increase as projects are accelerated. Each of the assumptions you made in your assumptions list has, based on history, a certain percentage chance of happening. Of course we do not have a crystal ball, so we do not know which surprise we will be hit with until it happens. We do know how many of these will manifest statistically. The more we accelerate critical paths, the more we lean heavily on these assumptions, and the more these negative (failure) assumptions become true. By the way, as we accelerate, the more paths become critical as well, exponentially increasing the costing. You should present management with not only the cost-benefit curves and figures of alternative schedules, but also the added risks and consequences. You don't want to sign up for the consequences— your management does.

Here are some more worksheets for your use.

Estimating Worksheet

TASK LIST, WORK BREAKDOWN STRUCTURE
Includes unexpected events and non-project time

Task	Estimate	Date Due	Description
1			
2			
3			
4			
5			
6			
7			
8			
9			
10			
11			
12			
13			
14			
15			
16			
17			
18			

Scheduling Worksheet

Critical Path Diagram

Scheduling Worksheet

Task list by expected date (GANTT)

Task	Expected Date	Description
1		
2		
3		
4		
5		
6		
7		
8		
9		
10		
11		
12		
13		
14		
15		
16		
17		
18		

Interruptions Worksheet

What stands in your way of getting the job done?

What are the issues?	What can I do about it?

TOOLS

We have been quite clear in Chapter 1 that electronic and software tools are not the 'end-all' in project management. From time to time, however, people come up to me and ask my advice on which tool to buy. Rather than give a recommendation or endorsement, I have a process model for picking the right tool for your company.

If you can, assign one person to each appropriate tool for the current project (or even different projects). Keep good notes as to what was easy and what was hard for the tool. Some tools are particularly good at initial definition and breakdowns, yet modification is difficult. Still others are excellent at crashing projects or multiple scenarios; however their output reporting might be limited. It is still true that there is not one specific product that does all things well. If it did, it would probably take an infinity of memory and disk space!

It is true, however, that companies have habits. Some companies are forever modifying schedules and changing events. Still others love to accelerate projects. Other companies want least-cost answers. Typically, the habit pattern for a company is independent of the project it is running. Therefore, one particular software tool will be best for the 'personality' of the company that it is running on. Let the tool that works best be your choice.

PROJECT CONTROLS

Based on what has been said in this and prior chapters, we can summarise:

- It is almost better to control a project than plan it without controls, if forced to make a choice. Amend the network constantly using tools.
- Pick tasks small enough so that you can notice progress via deliverables rather than 'fence-post' analogies.
- Practice MBWA (Management By Walking Around) to be sure you catch trouble before it starts, and concentrate on the critical paths first.
- Put key people on the critical path and trainees off that path.
- Use non-critical path people to make up for lateness on the critical path.
- Keep everyone else posted of everyone's business so people know where they can jump in and help without your detailed assistance.

14 Building the right product

Chapter 2 was about building the product right (doing a quality job). This chapter is building the right product (getting the requirements right). There is no sense, as explained in Chapter 2, of using high-quality techniques to construct a product that breaks down. In this chapter, we will see that there is also no sense in doing a 'quality' job, building a product that is breakdown free, when in fact it is the wrong product. A product that does not meet the needs of your customer or market is not useful.

The topic of understanding customer requirements can be quite involved, and yet there are some straightforward techniques of considerable value in making sure that the scope is correct, that it does not 'creep', and that the product meets customer needs.

BASIC REQUIREMENTS TECHNIQUES

Notice how the following applies also in families!

- The importance of spending extra time with the customer to understand true needs cannot be underestimated.
- The customer may or may not know their needs, they may only know their wants; you may need to discern the difference. True needs are based on their mission, not their technology, solutions or opinions.
- Work breakdown structures clarify detailed requirements or their omissions.

Despite our intentions, there are many ways in which we cloud the true requirements for building the right product. Ways of clarifying these follow.

Ambiguity of requirements

Ambiguity remains one of the largest problems to be solved in formulating and translating requirements. It occurs during:

- the problem formulation process;
- the requirements development process by customers;
- the translation of these into statements for use in product development; and
- understanding of the requirement statements themselves.

Gause and Weinberg* showed sources of ambiguity were due to errors in observation, recall, interpretation and understanding of problem statements. Most errors leading to ambiguity, both during requirements development and analysis, are due to:

- observation errors: failing to perceive correctly or paying inadequate attention to what is available;
- recall errors: failing to remember what was observed (whether correctly or incorrectly);
- interpretation errors: bringing an inappropriate meaning to what was seen or remembered; or
- problem statement misunderstanding: answering the wrong question or problem.

Users, liaisons and developers can identify much ambiguity, although perhaps not always rectify it, by using following four heuristics:

1   *Ambiguity poll and clustering heuristic*

- devise a quantitative problem to be solved by using methods in requirements;
- ask all customers, anticipated or not, to solve problem and compare answers; if results differ, one or more of above four errors have occurred;
- often, small answer variations about a 'cluster' are due to observation and recall errors; different clusters indicate interpretation or problem statement errors.

2   *Memorisation heuristic*

- tests for recall errors;
- many varied team members attempt to write key requirements verbatim from memory;
- differences usually are due to ambiguity or illogical conditions in requirements.

3   *Emphasis heuristic*

- emphasise different words in requirement and see if meaning shifts, and how.

4   *Definition heuristic*

- combine different dictionary definitions or maps for key words and explore the differences.

---

*   Donald C. Gause & Gerald M. Weinberg, *Exploring Requirements: Quality Before Design* pp102–3. Copyright © 1989 by Donald C. Gause and Gerald M. Weinberg (ISBN: 0-932633-13-7). Reprinted by permission of Dorset House Publishing, 353W.12 St. New York, NY 10014 (www.dorsethouse.com or 212-620-4053). All rights reserved.

Direct question alternatives*

During the interviewing technique, especially in technology areas, we may miss the customer's entire point and intent. This can happen because we are too direct with our questioning, and 'closed ended'. Therefore, we build the wrong product. Gauss and Weinberg* have illustrated some examples of alternatives to this narrow questioning technique, as shown below:

1   Context-free process questions

- Who is the client?
- What is a highly successful solution really worth to this client?
- What is the real reason for wanting to solve this problem?
- Should we use a single design team, or more than one?
- Who should be on the team(s)?
- How much time do we have for this project?
- What is your trade-off between time and value?
- Where else can the solution to this design problem be obtained?
- Can we copy something that already exists?

2   Context-free product questions

- What problems does this product solve?
- What problems could this product create?
- What environment is this product likely to encounter?
- What kind of precision is required or desired in the product?

3   Metaquestions

- Am I asking you too many questions?
- Do my questions seem relevant?
- Are you the right person to answer these questions?
- Are your answers official?
- Would you study and approve your written answers to my questions?
- Is there anything else I should be asking you?
- Is there anything you would like to ask me?
- May I return with more questions later?

---

*   Donald C. Gause & Gerald M. Weinberg, *Exploring Requirements: Quality Before Design* pp 65-7. Copyright © 1989 by Donald C. Gause and Gerald M. Weinberg (ISBN: 0-932633-13-7). Reprinted by permission of Dorset House Publishing, 353W.12 St. New York, NY 10014 (www.dorsethouse.com or 212-620-4053). All rights reserved.

- I notice you hesitated. Is there something else I should know?
- When I asked X about that, she said Y. How come she said Y?
- I notice you don't seem to agree. Would you tell me about that?
- Are you comfortable with the process right now?
- Is there any reason you don't feel you can answer freely?
- What can you tell me about the others on this project?
- How do you feel about the other people working on this project?
- Is there anyone we need on this project that we don't have?
- Is there anyone we have on this project that we don't need?

From vague to precise

You may be familiar, when working with others, about how to get precision in answers to your questions. Sometimes you are effective, and sometimes not. Fortunately, a model has been developed to categorise some of the ways in which people are instinctively fuzzy about what they say and want. This can be an excellent technique in identifying customer requirements.

We often do this in a number of ways. Here are some:

- Universals: all, never, every, each. These overused overbroad statements are often made, such as 'He never does this'. Your question is: Never? Is there ever one time when he has? What time was this? Under what circumstances?...
- Deletions, for example, 'I'm scared'. About what?
- The 'shoulds', including musts and can'ts. So, what would happen if you did, and what's stopping you?
- Vague verbs—get specifics. 'She really frustrates me'. In what way? How does she frustrate you?
- Vague nouns—get 'who' or 'what' specifics. 'They don't like me'. Who does not like you?
- Vague comparisons, such as too many, too much, too costly. 'That is a better approach.' Better than what? Compared to what else?

Exercise: Preciseness

(For groups) Form pairs.

Person one will be asking a series of questions about person two's job to get them to be more specific, using the model above.

Person two will tell person one what they want from their job.

In not more than 10–15 minutes, person one will ask as many as 100 questions of person two. Person two will give short one or two sentence answers with each sentence no longer than 10–15 words maximum.

Hint: If you have gone longer than 10–15 seconds between questions, you have been listening to long-winded answers and not asking enough questions!

Remember: You are not therapists! You are not suggesting an answer or reading minds; you are helping person two to focus on specifics.

Reforming vagueness: the Meta Model

There is an NLP model in even more detail than the general categories shown above, called the Meta Model. In somewhat medical language, it precisely categorises errors in language by name. For cases where you are getting extremely critical information, you may want to use this model (sparingly). Remember, interrogation may not be a great idea, or you might be called a Meta Monster! You can use questions without questioning, as we have covered in Chapter 9. In NLP this is called the Milton Model, named after Milton Ericson. It is explained in the following pages.

Meta Model violations

Generalisations, deletions, distortions

Gathering information:

- deletion
- comparative deletion
- lack of referential index
- unspecified verbs
- nominalisations

Expanding limiting generalisations:

- universal quantifiers

- modal operators of necessity/possibility

Exploring and reforming distortions

- cause-effect
- mind reading
- lost performative

In looking more intensively at ways that information is lost, we see three levels, moving from bad to worst: generalisations, deletions and distortions. Generalisations are overly sweeping statements, seldom completely true in the world. Deletions selectively pay attention to certain experiences and exclude others. Distortions are the worst because they shift our experience altogether.

In the first five points of the model, we want to gather more information.

- A deletion is a statement with missing information, such as 'I am happy'. About what?
- A comparative deletion misses the evaluation standard, meaning that one of the two objects being compared is dropped, such as 'That's a better object'. Better than what?
- A lack of referential index is, more simply, a pronoun that is unidentified, such as 'They don't work with my boss'. Who, specifically, doesn't work with the boss?
- An unspecified verb deletes specifics of when, where, or how, such as 'He sent me'. How did he send you? Where?
- A nominalisation is the noun clause we discussed in written communication in Chapter 10. It is a verb made into a noun, typically with -ment or -tion at the end, making it obscure, such as 'She wants entertainment'. How does she want to be entertained?

In the next two points of the model, we want to expand generalisations that are unnecessarily limiting. It is odd that things that are very sweeping are, in a sense, limiting; this is because their very inference excludes other possibilities.

- A universal quantifier is a generalisation that precludes other choices or exceptions because of its nature, such as 'He never gets the procedure right' Never? You mean there was never a time when he got it right? What would happen if he did?
- A modal operator of necessity / possibility, or simply the 'shoulds', are words that force a particular behaviour or imply no choice in the matter, such as 'You should read that book'. Who says you should?

In the final three points in the model, we explore and reform distortions into clarity.

- Cause-effect, seldom true in the world, profoundly implies that a particular stimulus causes a specific response, such as 'You make me do it'. How do I make you do it? In what way?
- Mind-reading is just that; assuming that you know what the other person is thinking, feeling, doing (without observing), such as 'I know you don't care about me'. How, specifically, do you know that?

- A lost performative, or simply missing authority figure, is a situation where the source of the value judgement or opinion is missing, such as 'It's a great way to fix it'. Who says it's great? How do you know it is great?

Quite detailed, to be sure; however, try your hand at the following poem, the last exercise of the book. As with most artistry, vagueness can be creative and expansive, and has its place. Our point is not to 'fix' this poem. However, every line in it has at least one, and sometimes more, Meta Model violations in it! I am indebted to the Southern Institute of NLP for this example. See if you can name the violations, and form the questions that would reform the clarity of it (if the poem's author were present).

Meta Model poem exercise

I'm sad and depressed.

Life is nothing but pain and suffering,

and the best way to deal with it

is to get enlightenment

because that's the truth

and people should see it,

but they never do,

and it blocks my energy

so I can't find my self,

and communication is crazy

but you know what I mean—

because we share the same space!

What do I do on Monday?

This closing chapter will help you make sense of the entire book, and to know what things to do, and in what order, and how not to be discouraged!

It may take you six months or a year to integrate all of the techniques and make them work for you. Based on the difficulty of managing change, you have learned that to try too much too fast would be an overload.

The USA's late president, John F. Kennedy, proposed an exercise program for US citizens. It was, 'Start slowly, build up gradually, and stick with it'. Good advice. I would recommend this same approach for implementing the ideas in this book.

In general, start applying the techniques in Section 2 before those of Section 3. You need to be a model for others before you can motivate others. A possible action plan for you, just as a sample, appears below. It is an illustration; feel free to re-arrange the topics in the way that suits you.

ACTION PLAN

1 Re-read Chapters 1, 2, 13 and 14.
2 In Chapter 3, log time usage for one week then stop.
3 Next week, look at the results, plus strengths worksheet.
4 Next week, put in some plans and re-run time log.
5 Next week, analyse the results.
6 Next week, swish pattern some changes.
7 In the week following, note the changes.
8 The following week, introduce daily planning model.
9 The week after, work on your real self.
10 Next week, practise daily thorough stress technique.
11 ...
12 ...
13 In Section 3, ...
14 ...

In other words, try one new topic a week until it integrates into habit. Then, start applying one by one the techniques in Section 3. These can be interleaved with those in Section 2 if desired, as long as the skill related to others is first worked on yourself. By this progressive escalation, you will succeed!

 Do what you can, and stay optimistic—good luck! I am sure you will have as much success with these activities as I have. And, above all, thank you for reading, and taking on this challenge in self-improvement. It has been a pleasure.

Index